Fingerprint Analysis Laboratory Workbook

Fingerprint Analysis Laboratory Workbook

Second Edition

Hillary Moses Daluz

CRC Press
Taylor & Francis Group
Boca Raton London New York

CRC Press is an imprint of the
Taylor & Francis Group, an **informa** business

CRC Press
Taylor & Francis Group
6000 Broken Sound Parkway NW, Suite 300
Boca Raton, FL 33487-2742

Printed on acid-free paper

International Standard Book Number-13: 978-1-138-48804-5 (Hardback)
International Standard Book Number-13: 978-1-138-48805-2 (Paperback)

Library of Congress Cataloging-in-Publication Data

Names: Daluz, Hillary Moses, author.
Title: Fingerprint analysis laboratory workbook / Hillary Moses Daluz.
Description: Second edition. | Boca Raton, FL: CRC Press, [2019] | Includes
bibliographical references and index.
Identifiers: LCCN 2018028488 | ISBN 9781138488045 (hardback: alk. paper) |
ISBN 9781138488052 (pbk.: alk. paper) | ISBN 9781351042185 (ebook) |
ISBN 9781351042154 (mobi/kindle)
Subjects: LCSH: Fingerprints. | Fingerprints—Identification. | Forensic sciences. | Criminal investigation.
Classification: LCC HV6074 .D352984 2019 | DDC 363.25/8—dc23
LC record available at https://lccn.loc.gov/2018028488

Visit the Taylor & Francis Web site at
http://www.taylorandfrancis.com

and the CRC Press Web site at
http://www.crcpress.com

Dedication

This work is dedicated to

Micah Alexander Daluz

Whose patience, optimism, and affectionate nature

inspire and motivate me every day

Contents

Part I Introduction to Fingerprints

Part II   Latent Print Development

Part III Fingerprint Analysis

List of Figures

Preface

In the pursuit of any scientific endeavor, the mastery of critical skills requires hands-on exploration and laboratory skills. Forensic science is unique in that it is practiced not only in the laboratory but also in the field. Fingerprint analysis may be performed as part of many job functions supporting law enforcement efforts: crime scene technician, latent print examiner, criminalist, latent print technician, forensic specialist, or forensic scientist. Regardless of the chosen career path, background knowledge of forensic scientific practices is critical for success. The best way to learn any science is to perform experiments and hands-on activities, in order to fully comprehend the principles and concepts learned in the classroom and in training.

The purpose of the *Fingerprint Analysis Laboratory Workbook, Second Edition,* is to provide the practitioner or student with a set of labs and exercises to put into practice the concepts learned in the accompanying text, *Fundamentals of Fingerprint Analysis, Second Edition.* The sequence of workbook and laboratory exercises in the *Fingerprint Analysis Laboratory Workbook, Second Edition,* is designed to parallel the textbook entitled *Fundamentals of Fingerprint Analysis, Second Edition.* The book chapters align with the laboratory exercises. For example, the laboratory exercises in Lab #13 correspond to the topics covered in Chapter 13 of the textbook. Many of the laboratory exercises may be completed either at home or in a laboratory setting.

Health and safety are of utmost importance when working in a laboratory. Wherever possible, the least toxic and most environmentally safe chemical reagents are recommended. Regardless, it is generally recommended to limit exposure and adhere to all safety precautions. Nitrile gloves and lab coats should be worn at all times. Safety glasses with side shields or chemical-resistant laboratory goggles protect the eyes. A particulate mask may be used to prevent inhalation of fingerprint powder particles. A fume hood is always used when working with chemical reagents.

All chemicals should be properly mixed, labeled, and stored in a cool, dry place away from open flames. Chemical storage containers should contain, at a minimum, the following information: chemical contents, preparer's initials, and the date. Flammable chemicals should be stored in a flammables cabinet. MSDS or SDS sheets for each reagent used should be available for reference. All chemicals should be disposed of according to Occupational Safety and Health Administration (OSHA) guidelines. Personal safety is a matter of proper education, due diligence, and common sense.

The second editions of these texts have been updated with the most recent research, concepts, and nomenclature in the field of fingerprint analysis. Paradigm shifts in the field have been presented along with emerging research and a look into the future of the science. There is also an international focus and an additional chapter addressing point counting, error rates, and statistics. The *Fingerprint Analysis Laboratory Workbook, Second Edition,* is beneficial for the education and professional development of forensic scientists, college students, legal experts, and law enforcement professionals.

This text utilizes American terminology and colloquialisms; however, it is intended for an international audience. The word "print" refers to any evidentiary friction ridge impression. This may be a palm print, fingerprint, or any other area of friction ridge skin. What is known as a "fingerprint" in the United States is referred to as a "fingermark" or "mark" throughout Europe and elsewhere in the world. "Record" prints—also referred to as exemplars or known prints—are prints that originate from a known source, such as inked prints taken on a tenprint card. A latent print "identification" is the determination that an evidentiary print and a record print may have originated from the same source.

Similarly, friction ridge development techniques vary from country to country. The decisions a fingerprint analyst makes when it comes to selection and sequence of chemical reagents are region dependent. A technique that works well in Virginia may not work, or be available, in the United Kingdom, and vice versa. Atmospheric and laboratory conditions such as temperature, pressure, and humidity, as well as storage and handling, can affect the success of a particular reagent. Wherever possible, international research is presented and discussed.

The second edition of the accompanying laboratory manual entitled *Fingerprint Analysis Laboratory Workbook* is intended to enhance the topics addressed in the textbook. The textbook chapters align with the laboratory exercises. The laboratory exercises, introductory materials, and post lab questions give students hands-on experience and supplemental information that enhances comprehension.

Both editions include teaching tools not found in other professional forensics texts, such as case studies, chapter review questions, chapter summaries, and introductory scientific material. They also incorporate optional instructor materials such as PowerPoint lectures for each chapter, a bank of test questions for each chapter, answers to review questions, and other useful teaching tools that are beneficial to forensic science students and professionals, criminal justice professionals, attorneys, and laypersons.

I trust the second edition of *Fundamentals of Fingerprint Analysis* will benefit forensic scientists, college students, legal experts, and law enforcement professionals as much as authoring it has furthered my professional development.

Acknowledgments

This project would not have been possible without the love and support of my family. To my husband, Norberto Daluz: I cannot thank you enough for your optimism, support, and advocacy. To my son, Micah: not many three-year-olds would be as understanding as you when mommy would write at all hours of the day instead of playing trains and cars. I would like to thank my mom, Susan Moses, for her tireless and meticulous editing and for inspiring me as a teacher and as a mom. And to my dad, Ken Moses: you are my mentor, my advocate, and my favorite colleague. Your passion for science both inspired me to follow in your footsteps and encouraged me to forge my own path.

Thank you to my editor, Mark Listewnik: thank you for spearheading this project and working tirelessly to promote my books. Thank you also to Misha Kydd for answering dozens of questions during the writing process.

I am honored to have had a distinguished group of colleague proofreaders as a part of this project's first edition: Ken Moses, Robert Ramotowski, Robert Gaensslen, Mike Stapleton, Mark Hawthorne, Wilson Sullivan, David Burow, Kathy and Peter Higgins, Kasey Wertheim, Kimberlee Sue Moran, Helen Gourley, Malory Green, David Haymer, and Ron Smith.

Thank you to the colleagues who have mentored, educated, and inspired me, especially the members of the International Association for Identification who nurtured my career from its inception.

Finally, I would like to acknowledge my colleagues worldwide—many deployed to battlefield environments—working tirelessly to make our communities safer places to live.

About the Author

Hillary Moses Daluz is an instructor for Tri Tech Forensics and a Forensic Specialist with Forensic Identification Services. Daluz began her career as a Police Identification Specialist with the City of Hayward Police Department in Hayward, California. After earning her Masters of Science degree in Forensic Science from the University of California, Davis, she deployed to the Joint Expeditionary Forensic Facility at Camp Victory in Baghdad, Iraq, as a Latent Print Examiner. After returning stateside, she became a member of the faculty in the Forensic Sciences program at Chaminade University of Honolulu. She then accepted a position as a Senior Latent Print Technician with American Systems. Daluz serves on the Board of Directors for the International Association for Identification.

Part I

Introduction to Fingerprints

Chapter 1

Introduction
Class and Individual Characteristics

Objectives

- Understand the concept of class and individual characteristics and how this applies to the science of fingerprint identification
- Identify the class and individual characteristics of fingerprints

1.1 Background

Any effort to organize and categorize a large group of items begins with observation. Large groups of things are often organized based on visible characteristics such as color, size, type, or material. Observable features used to organize a large group of things into smaller categories are known as *class characteristics*. Forensic evidence such as trace evidence utilizes class characteristics to determine whether a fiber, hair, or soil sample is consistent with similar material from a crime scene. While a fiber does not contain individualizing characteristics such as DNA, it does contain class characteristics such as length, color, material (natural or synthetic), and cross-sectional shape. A comparison of class characteristics from evidentiary fibers and fibers from a suspect's home, car, or clothing can elucidate an association between the suspect and the crime scene but cannot conclusively determine the origin of the fibers.

For example, vehicles can exhibit both class and individualizing characteristics. They can be organized by make, model, color, or type. Individualizing characteristics organize items into a category of one. For example, individual characteristics of a vehicle may include specific body damage (dents, scratches), a VIN number, or a license plate number. While many vehicles may share class attributes of color, make, and model, only one vehicle will have these individualizing characteristics.

Forensic scientists distinguish between class and individual characteristics of forensic evidence in order to organize large amounts of data or determine the potential source of evidentiary materials. If a single hair with a root attached is found at a crime scene, the potential source of that hair may be determined with an analysis of class and individualizing characteristics. People may have black, brown, blonde, or red hair. While the source of that hair cannot be identified based on class characteristics alone—such as hair color, eye color, or ethnic origin—it can narrow the potential source or eliminate a subject. In order to further narrow down the source of the hair, one would need to conduct a DNA analysis. Similarly, friction ridge impressions provide individualizing characteristics that can narrow down the potential source of forensic evidence to a category of one.

Friction ridge impressions contain both class and individual characteristics. Pattern types are class characteristics, because they are not unique to an individual. There are three main pattern types: arches, loops, and whorls. Within those categories are eight subcategories: plain arches, tented arches, ulnar loops, radial loops, plain whorls, double-loop whorls, central pocket loop whorls, and accidentals (Figure 1.1). Most

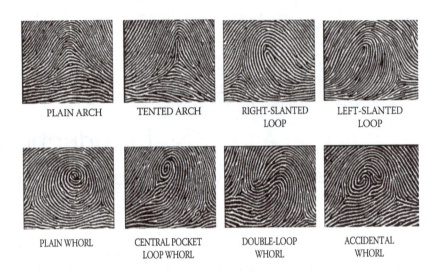

Figure 1.1
The eight fingerprint sub-pattern types: plain arch, tented arch, right-slanted loop, left-slanted loop, plain whorl, central pocket loop whorl, double-loop whorl, and accidental whorl.

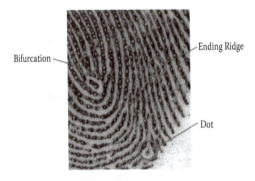

Figure 1.2
A bifurcation, dot, and ending ridge in a magnified portion of a fingerprint.

fingerprints in the population are loop patterns, while whorls are much less common, and arches are rare. Finding a latent print with an arch pattern at a crime scene is valuable for elimination purposes, because they are so rare in the population. Conversely, finding a latent print with a loop pattern at a crime scene is not as discriminating, because loops are very common in the population.

While pattern types can be used to narrow down the population of fingerprints or eliminate a subject as the possible contributor of a latent print, they do not have individualizing power. Minutiae are individualizing characteristics. They can be used to narrow down the potential source of a latent print. There are three types of fingerprint minutiae: bifurcations, ending ridges, and dots (Figure 1.2). While all individuals have ending ridges and bifurcations present along friction ridges, an analysis of the relative locations of those minutiae in the impression makes it possible to identify the potential source of a latent print. An analysis of both the class characteristics (pattern types, ridge flow, level 3 detail) and individual characteristics (minutiae types and relative locations) contribute to fingerprint identification. In the following laboratory exercises, you will explore the class and individual characteristics of various types of forensic evidence as well as the three types of fingerprint minutiae.

1.2 Materials

- Pen or pencil
- Figure 1.3
- Figure 1.4

1.3 Exercises

Part I: Class and Individual Characteristics

1. Identify the class and individual characteristics for each type of forensic evidence listed in Figure 1.3.

Part II: Class Characteristics

1. Identify all observable class characteristics of a classmate, friend, colleague, or spouse
2. What are the individualizing characteristics associated with that individual?

Evidence	Class Characteristics	Individual Characteristics
Fiber		
Hair		
Blood		
Fingerprint		
Shoeprint		

Figure 1.3
Part I: Class and Individual Characteristics—Identify the class and individual characteristics for each type of forensic evidence listed.

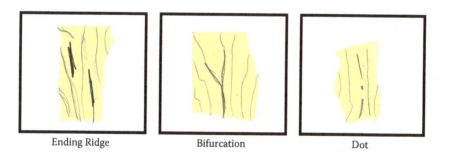

Ending Ridge   Bifurcation   Dot

Figure 1.4
Part III: Individualizing Characteristics—minutiae: draw a bifurcation, ending ridge, and dot.

Part III: Individualizing Characteristics—Minutiae

1. Draw the following minutiae in Figure 1.4:
   a. Bifurcation
   b. Ending ridge
   c. Dot

1.4 Post-Lab Questions

1. Are fingerprint pattern types individual characteristics? Why or why not?
2. What are the eight fingerprint sub-pattern types?
3. What are the three types of minutiae found in fingerprints?
4. Are minutiae class or individual characteristics? Why or why not?
5. Besides narrowing the possible source of a fingerprint, what is another use for class characteristic determination?

Chapter

History

Objectives

- Know the importance of understanding the history behind the science of fingerprint analysis
- Explore anthropometric methods of personal identification

2.1 Background

Many historical figures have contributed to the development of fingerprint analysis as a scientific discipline. It is important to be able to identify key historical figures and their contributions to fingerprint analysis. It is also important to understand the history in order to understand future scientific developments in context. A fingerprint analyst may be asked about the history of the science in a court of law. Having this knowledge enhances the analyst's credibility. Historical questions may also arise during professional certification and proficiency tests. Proficiency tests are tests given to professionals at regular intervals (often yearly) that assess the examiner's knowledge and fitness for case work. Certification tests must be passed in order for the professional to be formally certified in a given forensic sub-discipline, such as tenprint examination or latent print examination. Certification carries experiential and training requirements that must be met before the exam is taken.

Fingerprints were used to mark ancient pottery and acted both as a signature mark of the potter as well as decoration for the exterior of the vessel. It is likely the first use of fingerprints as identifying marks was during the Qin and Han dynasties in China (246 BCE).[1] Fingerprints and palm prints were used on official documents including marriage documents, land deeds, army rosters, and records of indenture.[1] The most influential historical figures who contributed to the development of fingerprint analysis are listed below, in chronological order:

- Nehemiah Grew (1684)—examined fingerprints under the early microscope and published a paper based on his observations[2]
- Marcello Malpighi (late 1600s)—published a paper about his microscopic observations of friction ridges and described the evolutionary function and importance of friction ridge structures[3]
- Johannes Purkinje—made detailed observations and line drawings of friction ridge patterns[4]
- Sir William Herschel—magistrate and collector in British-controlled India used palm prints to authenticate contracts; fingerprinted himself over a period of 50 years to demonstrate the persistence of friction ridge formations[4]
- JCA Mayer (1788)—published the idea that fingerprints are unique structures[5]
- Dr. Henry Faulds (1880)—published the idea that fingerprints could be used to solve crimes[4]
- Sir Francis Galton (1892)—published the first book on friction ridge structures entitled *Finger Prints*; described minutiae; described friction ridge features as unique and permanent[5]
- Alphonse Bertillon—originated a method of anthropometric classification for criminal record keeping known as *Bertillonage*
- Juan Vucetich (1904)—developed the first system of alphanumeric fingerprint classification used in Spanish-speaking countries[5]

- Sir Edward Henry—developed the first system of alphanumeric fingerprint classification used in English-speaking countries[5]

These individuals and many others contributed to the development of the science of fingerprints over the past three-and-a-half centuries.

Along with the individual scientists who contributed to furthering fingerprint analysis, several scientific developments caused paradigm shifts in the field. The first major development was the concept of classification. As criminal records became more numerous, it was necessary to devise a method for organizing the existing records and searching for duplicate records. One of the first methods of criminal identification was anthropometry: the identification of an individual using biological measurements. Bertillonage—named for Alphonse Bertillon—was the name given to the anthropometric method of identification and classification of arrestees. Measurements of body features such as the head, ears, arms, and legs were compiled on a card known as a *Bertillonage card*. This card featured a photograph (what we now call a "mug shot") surrounded by anthropometric measurements (Figure 2.1).

Anthropometry was abandoned in the early nineteenth century because it was not a reliable method of individualization. It is possible for two individuals who are similar in appearance to have similar measurements. Fingerprints, however, are a reliable form of individualization. Fingerprint cards replaced Bertillonage cards as the primary records of criminal identification and classification and are still the preferred criminal records in use today.

Modern fingerprint analysis has benefited from several paradigm shifts in the field. In 1973, the International Association for Identification published the statement that there was no scientific basis for a minimum point standard when comparing two friction ridge impressions.[6] This changed the culture and approach to fingerprint identification in the United States. Over the next two decades, many other countries followed suit and abolished the minimum point standard though some still maintain that approach.

In the 1980s, the advent of the silicone chip led to the development of the Automated Fingerprint Identification System (AFIS), a computer that could store and search fingerprints digitally. This resulted in a

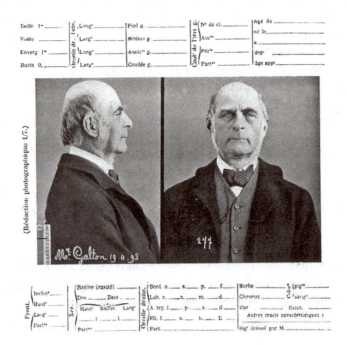

Figure 2.1
Sir Francis Galton's Bertillonage card was recorded when Galton paid a visit to Alphonse Bertillon's laboratory in 1893.

significant decrease in crimes, especially property crimes. A judicial decision in the 1990s resulted in a new standard for the admissibility of scientific testimony. Known as the *Daubert decision*, it caused a wave of criticism of the forensic sciences, the consequence of which was renewed scientific vigor in the fingerprint sciences.

Most recently, the 2009 National Academy of Sciences (NAS) publication entitled *Strengthening Forensic Science in the United States: A Path Forward* made several recommendations for improving forensic sciences, which resulted in a wave of research that has significantly enhanced the science of fingerprint examination.[7] The following exercises address both the early and recent historical developments that have molded fingerprint examination into the science we know today.

2.2 Materials

- Figure 2.2
- Digital camera
- Computer
- Printer
- Scissors
- Tape or glue
- Measuring implements (tape measure, ruler, cloth measuring tape)
- Pen or pencil

2.3 Exercises

Part I: Anthropometry—Bertillonage Cards

1. Take a digital photograph of your laboratory partner (head and shoulders).
2. Upload the photograph to a computer.

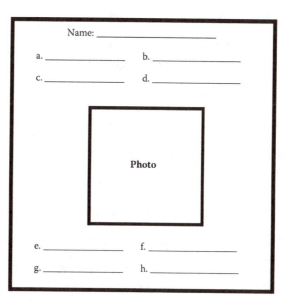

Figure 2.2

Part I: Anthropometry—Bertillonage Cards: create your own Bertillonage cards with a photo and anthropomorphic measurements.

3. Resize the photograph to 1.25″×1.25″ and print it out.
4. Cut and adhere the photo to the center of the Bertillonage card (Figure 2.2).
5. Record the following anthropometric measurements on Figure 2.2:
   a. Height
   b. Length of the ear
   c. Width of the ear
   d. Length of the right little finger
   e. Measurement of wingspan (from the left middle finger to the right middle finger when the arms are held parallel to the ground)
   f. Length of the left index finger
   g. Length of the left forearm
   h. Length of the left foot

Part II: Paradigm Shifts

1. Consider the major events that have resulted in a paradigm shift in your life
2. Write out the major events that have changed the course of your life and share with a partner.

2.4 Post-Lab Questions

1. Why is it important to know the historical figures behind the development of fingerprint analysis?
2. What is Bertillonage?
3. Compare your anthropometric measurements with those of your classmates. Do any two individuals have the same or similar measurements?
4. Why is Bertillonage inferior to fingerprints for recording and classifying criminal records?
5. What were the paradigm shifts that shaped the modern course of fingerprint analysis?

References

1. Xiang-Xin, Z. and Chun-Ge, L. 1998. The historical application of hand prints in Chinese litigation. *J. Forensic Ident.* 38(6): 277–284.
2. Grew, N. 1684. The description and use of the pores in the skin of the hands and feet. *Philos. Trans. R. Soc. Lond.* 14: 566–567.
3. Barnes, J. 2011. History. In *The Fingerprint Sourcebook*. U.S. Department of Justice, Office of Justice Programs. Washington, DC: National Institute of Justice.
4. Berry, J. and Stoney, D. 2001. History and development of fingerprinting. In Lee, H. and Gaensslen, R.E. (Eds.), *Advances in Fingerprint Technology*, 2nd edn. Boca Raton, FL: Taylor & Francis.
5. Ashbaugh, D. 1999. Quantitative-Qualitative Friction Ridge Analysis: An Introduction to Basic and Advanced Ridgeology. Boca Raton, FL: Taylor & Francis.
6. Resolutions and Legislative Committee. 1973. *Resolution 1973–1975*. International Association for Identification. August, 1973. www.theiai.org/member/resolutions/1973/Resolution_1973-5.pdf (accessed March 1, 2018).
7. Committee on Identifying the Needs of the Forensic Sciences Community, National Research Council. 2009. *Strengthening Forensic Science in the United States: A Path Forward*. Document No. 228091. National Academy of Sciences. Washington, DC: United States Department of Justice.

Chapter 3

Physiology and Embryology

Objectives

- Understand the embryological development of friction ridges
- Understand the proliferation of friction ridges and minutiae in the developing friction ridge skin of the hands and feet

3.1 Background

Friction ridge skin forms between the sixth and 25th week of fetal development. Prior to friction ridge formation, volar pads form on the palmar and plantar region of the fetal hand and foot (Figure 3.1). Volar pads are swellings of skin that regress as friction ridge development begins. As the volar pads recede, friction ridges begin to proliferate across the surface of the skin. As they spread out, minutiae form as follows: friction ridges that abruptly end create ending ridges; ridges that split into two create bifurcations; single ridge units that do not have time to form and extend create dots.

Fingerprints are effective for identification, because they are both unique and persistent. They are unique because friction ridge skin forms *in utero* and is influenced by a multitude of developmental processes including genetics, the mother's nutrition, the position of the fetus, the fetal environment, growth stresses, the topography and thickness of the developing skin, bone formation and morphology, and the timing and rate of ridge maturation.[1-6] This results in true uniqueness of friction ridge skin.

Fingerprints are considered persistent because the blueprint for the friction ridge skin (including the positions of minutiae) is set for life in the deepest epidermal layer of the skin before birth. The blueprint layer of skin is one cell thick and is known as the *basal layer* (Figure 3.2). If the basal layer is cut, the blueprint of friction ridges is interrupted and a scar will be visible on the surface of the skin. In this laboratory exercise, you will explore the proliferation of friction ridges and the embryological development of fingerprint minutiae.

3.2 Materials

- Safety glasses
- White or light-colored rubber balloons (deflated)
- Black permanent marker
- Medium binder clip
- Figure 3.5
- Blank sheet of 8.5 ×11″ white paper

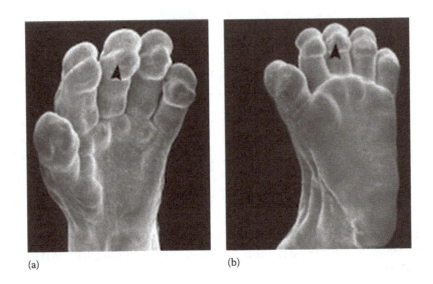

(a)   (b)

Figure 3.1
Scanning electron micrographs of the human embryonic hand (a) and foot (b) at the end of the second month of development. The volar pads are indicated with black arrows. (Reprinted with permission from Carlson, Bruce M., *Human Embryology and Developmental Biology*, (Elsevier: Oxford, 2014), Figure 9.4.)

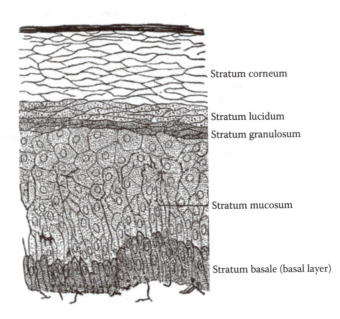

Stratum corneum

Stratum lucidum
Stratum granulosum

Stratum mucosum

Stratum basale (basal layer)

Figure 3.2
The five layers of the epidermis—Stratum corneum, stratum lucidium, stratum granulosum, stratum mucosum, and stratum basale. (From Lewis, *Gray's Anatomy, 20th Edition*, 1918.)

3.3 Exercises

Part I: Embryological Development of Friction Ridges

1. Inflate a balloon to approximately the size of an orange.
2. Twist the bottom of the balloon and clip it with a binder clip to keep it inflated.

Figure 3.3
Part I: Embryological Development of Friction Ridges—A simple hand-drawn fingerprint pattern (step 3).

Figure 3.4
Part I: Embryological Development of Friction Ridges—A simple hand-drawn fingerprint pattern (step 5).

3. Hold the balloon vertically. On the side of the balloon, draw a simple fingerprint pattern (as in Figure 3.3) with a permanent marker. The "core" of the fingerprint pattern should be located in the center, approximately halfway up the side of the balloon.

4. Inflate the balloon to approximately the size of a grapefruit and secure it with the binder clip.

5. Add more ridges and fill in the spaces between the original ridges by both extending existing ridges and drawing in short ridges, bifurcations, and ending ridges. Try to keep the new friction ridges equidistant from the existing ridges (as in Figure 3.4).

6. Inflate the balloon completely and tie the base of the balloon to prevent it from deflating.

7. Add to the friction ridge pattern as in step 5.

Part II: Friction Ridge Unit Puzzle

1. Cut out the friction ridge units in Figure 3.5

2. Arrange the friction ridge units into friction ridges in any desired formation (with or without minutiae such as dots, bifurcations, or ending ridges).

3. Compare the results of your "friction ridges" with those of your colleagues.

4. How many different friction ridge formations were created? Do any two look exactly the same?

Chapter 5

Known Fingerprints

Objectives

- Understand the importance of taking comprehensive exemplar prints
- Thoroughly and accurately record known fingerprints using ink and powder

5.1 Background

Known fingerprints, otherwise referred to as exemplars, are fingerprints and palm prints recorded with powder, ink, or digitally. They are called *known prints*, because we know the origin of the fingerprints. Known fingerprints are recorded for several reasons.

1. As an official record of identity
2. To compare with latent prints
3. To determine whether an individual has a prior arrest
4. To serve as a record for subsequent searches

Exemplars must be comprehensive and of good quality because they are the records against which latent fingerprints will be searched. Latent fingerprints and palm prints may be found on evidentiary items or at crime scenes; therefore, palm print exemplars should also be recorded. The most comprehensive records of friction ridge skin include fingers, palms, the writer's palm (side of the hand), the joints, tips, and sides of fingers. The resulting exemplars are referred to as major case prints.

Ink was the most common medium for recording exemplars. Known prints were commonly recorded onto 8″×8″ printed white cards known as tenprint cards. The tenprint card contains demographic information and the rolled fingerprints of each finger. In order to capture the entire area of friction ridge skin, each finger is rolled in ink from the extreme left side of the finger (at the left side of the fingernail) to the extreme right side of the finger (at the right side of the fingernail). Fingerprints rolled from nail to nail appear square in shape (Figure 5.1).

The tenprint card also includes boxes to record the "flats" of the fingers. These fingerprints are not rolled. Instead, the four fingers of each hand are recorded simultaneously in the corresponding boxes on the tenprint card. The flats of the thumbs are also recorded on the card (Figure 5.2). It is important to use a light layer of ink and to roll the subject's finger with medium, even pressure. Too much pressure or ink can cause the ink to coat not only the friction ridges, but also the furrows between the ridges. The resulting rolled fingerprints appear smeared and indistinct. Using too much pressure causes distortion.

Fingerprint powder is another medium used to record friction ridge skin. One method for recording powdered exemplars is to use white adhesive sheets known as the Handiprint System® (available from CSI Forensic Supply). The resulting major case prints exhibit exceptional detail. The friction ridge edge shapes, pores, and fine creases are all visible. This level of detail is critical for the comparison process if the latent

Figure 5.1
Fingerprints rolled from nail to nail on a tenprint card should appear square in shape.

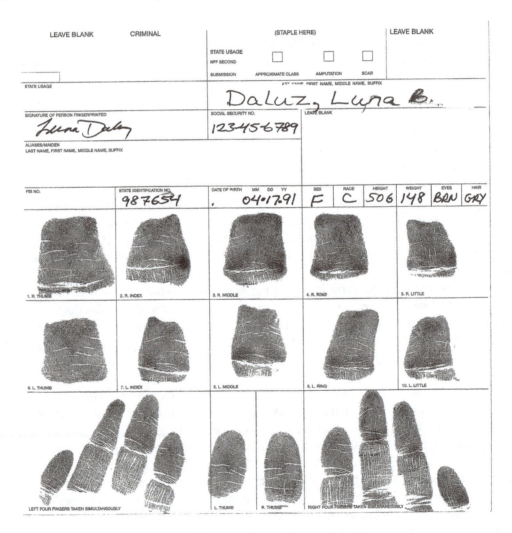

Figure 5.2
Tenprint card.

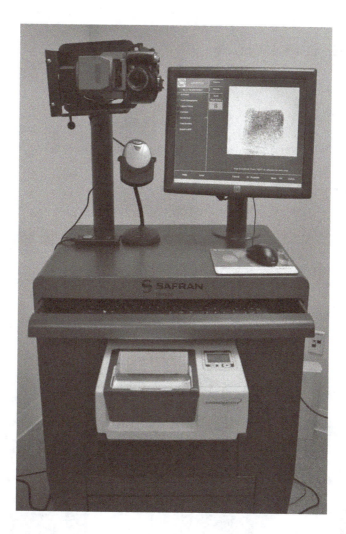

Figure 5.3
Livescan machine.

print displays pores, edge shapes, or creases. The powder method is also used to collect fingerprints from deceased persons, as it is difficult to roll a decedent's fingers with ink.

Most exemplars are recorded digitally. Digital fingerprint records do not require ink, powder, or any other medium other than a digital scanner to capture the exemplars. The fingerprints are scanned on a livescan device, which acquires the image on a glass platen similar to a document scanner. The resultant image then appears on the computer screen in a tenprint card format (Figure 5.3). Livescan devices directly connect to AFIS. Digital exemplars have quality controls, are instantly transmitted via computer networks, and can be stored on computers rather than as hard copies in filing cabinets. Regardless of the method used to record known fingerprints, the individual taking the prints must take great care to record comprehensive friction ridge impressions in order to maximize their forensic value.

5.2 Materials

- Pen
- Gloves
- Lab coat

- Safety glasses
- Ink pad (or a light layer of ink rolled out onto a glass slab)
- Tenprint card
- Fingerprint card holder
- Hand cleaner/wet wipes
- Permanent marker
- Handiprint System® (8″×8″ white adhesive sheets and acetate covers)
- Black fingerprint powder
- Standard fingerprint brush

5.3 Exercises

Part I: Inked Exemplars

1. Fill in the demographic information at the top of the tenprint card.
2. Secure the card in the cardholder so the first row of boxes is clearly visible (Figure 5.4).
3. Take control of your partner's right hand.

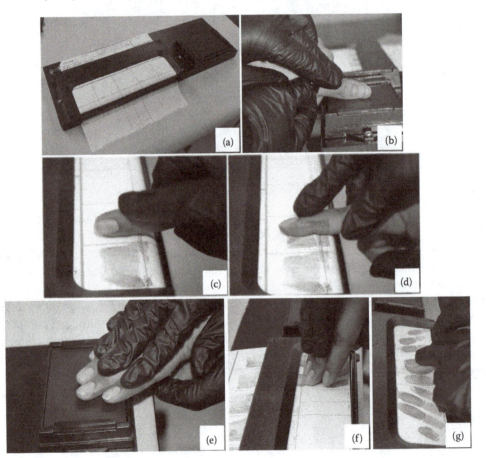

Figure 5.4
When recording a tenprint card, secure the card in the cardholder so the first row of boxes is clearly visible.

4. Roll a thin layer of ink onto the right thumb from nail to nail with light, even pressure.

5. Roll the right thumb from nail to nail onto the corresponding box on the tenprint card (labeled "1. R. Thumb") with light, even pressure.

6. Repeat with the remaining nine fingers.

7. Ink the flats of the four fingers simultaneously and roll the fingers upward to ink the tips of the fingers.

8. Press the four fingers onto the section of the card labeled "right four fingers taken simultaneously" and roll the fingers upward to record the tips of the fingers.

9. Press the right thumb lightly to the inkpad and roll the thumb upward to ink the tip of the thumb.

10. Press the right thumb to the area designated for the thumb flats (labeled "R. Thumb") and roll it upward to record the ridge detail at the tip of the thumb.

11. Repeat this procedure for the left hand.

Part II: Powdered Exemplars

1. Peel the backing off of the Handiprint System® white adhesive sheet and place it on the table with the adhesive side facing up (Figure 5.5).

2. Dip the fingerprint brush in black fingerprint powder and shake or twirl to remove the excess powder from the bristles.

3. Coat your lab partner's fingers, fingertips, finger joints, sides of the fingers, palm, and writer's palm with a light layer of fingerprint powder.

4. Press the powdered hand to the adhesive sheet with fingers spread apart.

5. With the sheet still adhered to the hand, turn the hand over and press the adhesive sheet to every section of the palm, finger joints, sides of finger joints, fingers, sides of fingers, and fingertips.

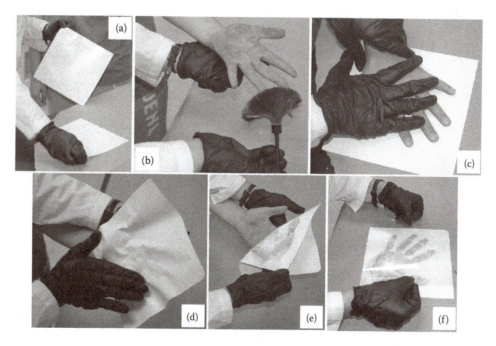

Figure 5.5
Powdered exemplars recorded with the Handiprint System®.

6. Peel the adhesive sheet from the hand and place the powdered print adhesive side up on the table.

7. Place the clear acetate cover over the powdered print on the adhesive sheet, taking care to avoid trapping air bubbles.

8. Record the subject's demographic information on the back of the exemplar.

5.4 Post-Lab Questions

1. What are the advantages of capturing digital fingerprints using a livescan device?

2. Why are inked fingerprints rolled from nail to nail?

3. Why is it important to use a light layer of ink and apply the fingerprint to the tenprint card with light, even pressure?

4. Observe the inked exemplars and powdered exemplars collected in this lab. How do the powdered fingerprint exemplars appear different from the inked fingerprint exemplars?

5. What fingerprint sub-pattern types are present?

Chapter 6

The Nature of Latent Prints

Objectives

- Understand the complexity and flow of ridges in a latent print
- Locate and count minutiae

6.1 Background

The three types of prints found at crime scenes or on evidentiary items are patent prints, plastic prints, and latent prints. Patent prints are visible to the human eye. They are friction ridge impressions in a visible medium. Bloody fingerprints and greasy fingerprints are examples of patent prints. Plastic prints are three-dimensional "molds" of friction ridges impressed into soft material, such as tacky paint, wax, or clay.

Latent prints are invisible and of unknown origin. They are created when a matrix (composed of sweat and other substances coating the friction ridges) is deposited on a substrate (surface) in the same way a pattern on a rubber stamp is replicated with ink. Pores on the friction ridges excrete eccrine sweat, which originates from eccrine glands deep in the dermis. The dermis is the deep layer of the skin below the epidermis. Eccrine sweat is composed mostly of water but also contains inorganic and organic compounds including lipids, fatty acids, proteins, and amino acids. When an individual touches the face or hair, body oils coat the friction ridges. Latent prints may also be composed of other contaminants handled during the normal course of a day include lotion, cosmetics, food, soap, or grease.

Substrates vary in texture and contour. They may be porous or nonporous, smooth or rough, flat or curved. Porous surfaces absorb a majority of the latent print matrix, while on nonporous surfaces the latent print matrix adheres to the surface. It is not possible to determine the age of a latent print. There are many factors that contribute to how long a latent print will persist on a surface including the chemical composition of the latent print, the nature and condition of the substrate, and the environment.

When a patent, plastic, or latent print is deposited on a surface, it often appears distorted when compared with the exemplar print. This is due to the elasticity of skin, motion, and deposition pressure involved with handling an object or touching a surface and the condition of the substrate. While the friction ridge impression may appear stretched, twisted, or have areas that are obscured, the relative positions and arrangement of minutiae will be consistent.

In this laboratory exercise, you will explore the flow of friction ridges as well as minutiae in enlarged fingerprints.

6.2 Materials

- Pencil
- Eraser

- Tracing paper
- Tape
- Figure 6.1
- Pen
- Red marker
- Figure 6.2

6.3 Exercises

Part I: The Structure of a Latent Print

1. Cut out a 3″×3″ square of tracing paper.
2. Secure the tracing paper over the enlarged fingerprint image (Figure 6.1) along the top edge using one small strip of tape.
3. Beginning on the outer edges of the print and working in, trace the ridges visible through the tracing paper.
4. Remove the tracing paper and compare your tracing with that of your lab partner by lining up the friction ridges and examining similarities and differences.

Part II: Minutiae in a Latent Print

1. On the enlarged image of a powdered fingerprint (Figure 6.2), indicate the pattern type.
2. Mark all visible fingerprint minutiae with red dots using a red marker. (For example, you would put a red dot at the end of an ending ridge or where a ridge bifurcates to form two ridges.)
3. Count and record the number of minutiae found.
4. Compare and contrast this number with your lab partner and discuss any minutiae that were or were not selected.

Figure 6.1
Enlarged image of an inked fingerprint.

Figure 6.2
Enlarged image of a powdered fingerprint.

6.4 Post-Lab Questions

1. Name and describe the three types of friction ridge impressions found at crime scenes and on evidentiary items.
2. What is a latent print?
3. What are the components of the latent print matrix?
4. Upon completion of Part I, were there any differences between the fingerprint tracings?
5. What features of a fingerprint other than minutiae are observed in Figure 6.2?

Chapter 7

Biometrics
Livescan and AFIS

Objectives

- Understand the role of biometrics in the forensic sciences
- Understand how the Automated Fingerprint Identification System (AFIS) searches tenprint and latent print databases
- Recognize the role of the latent print examiner (LPE) in conducting latent print searches

7.1 Background

Biometrics (from the root words *bio* meaning "life" and *metric* meaning "measure") refers to using biological measurements for identification purposes. A historical example of biometrics is anthropometry, in which measurements of specific parts of the body were used for criminal records, classification, and identification. There are several examples of forensic biometrics that rely on the unique characteristics of individuals for identification. Forensic odontologists (forensic dentists) analyze the unique shapes and placement of teeth, as well as dental work, in order to determine whether an unknown set of teeth belong to a particular source. Facial recognition involves an examination of the unique measurements, proportions, and features of the face and skin. Iris scans capture the unique patterns within the pigmented section of the eye. The forensic sciences rely on these and other biometrics to identify individuals.

Fingerprints are the most common biometric used for criminal identification. They were also the first biometrics to be recorded, stored, and searched via computer. Forensic scientists and criminal justice professionals utilize the AFIS to store criminal fingerprint and palm print records, perform background checks, determine if an individual has been arrested before, and search for possible matches to latent prints. The LPE enters a latent into the AFIS computer by scanning or photographing the print. The LPE may enhance the print and indicate which direction is up, which finger, hand, or portion of the palm to search, and where a core or delta is located. The LPE then either chooses minutiae or verifies the minutiae automatically selected by the computer (Figure 7.1).

Feature extraction is the process by which the computer reduces the print to only its minutiae (similar to a connect-the-dots puzzle) in order to search the database for a similar pattern of features (Figure 7.2). The computer sees only the minutiae not the friction ridges. It is programmed with an algorithm (a set of instructions and calculations for the computer to follow) that recognizes and codes (selects) minutiae. The latent is then searched in the computer's database of hundreds, thousands, or even millions of tenprint records. The computer returns a list of candidate fingerprints that have similar features in similar spatial positions. The LPE compares the original latent print image to the candidates' tenprint cards to determine whether they originated from the same source. In this laboratory exercise, you will act as the AFIS system by copying a fingerprint and performing feature extraction.

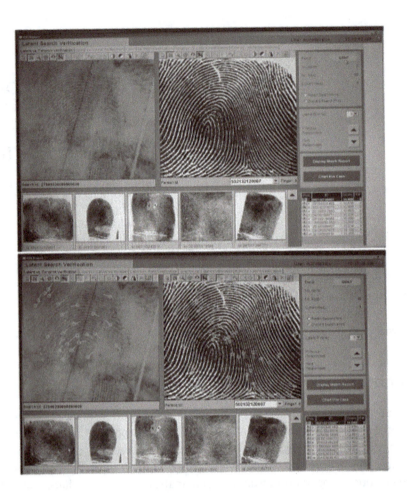

Figure 7.1
A latent print search on an AFIS computer.

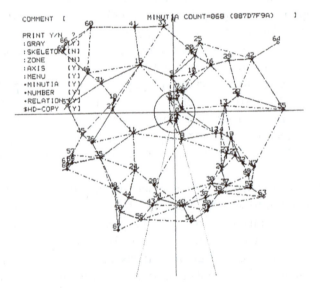

Figure 7.2
Feature extraction is the process by which the computer reduces the print to only its minutiae in order to search the database for a similar pattern of features.

7.2 Materials

- Pencil
- Eraser
- Tracing paper
- Tape
- Figure 7.3
- Red marker

7.3 Exercise

Part I: Feature Extraction—What Does the Computer See?

1. Cut out square of tracing paper slightly larger than Figure 7.3.
2. Secure the tracing paper over the enlarged fingerprint image (Figure 7.3) along the top edge using one small strip of tape.
3. Beginning on the outer edges of the print and working in, trace the ridges lightly in pencil.
4. Remove the tracing paper from Figure 7.3.
5. Mark all visible minutiae on the tracing paper with red dots.
6. Erase the pencil tracing.

Part II: Biometrics

1. There are at least 15 different types of biometric identification. Perform an Internet search to list and describe 15 or more biometrics.

Figure 7.3
Enlarged image of an inked fingerprint.

7.4 Post-Lab Questions

1. What is biometrics?

2. How are latent fingerprints searched in the AFIS computer?

3. In the above exercise, when you traced the fingerprint onto the tracing paper, located the minutiae, and compared the minutiae with your lab partner, you were recreating the functions of the AFIS computer. What AFIS function does the act of tracing the fingerprint represent?

4. What AFIS function does the selection of minutiae and erasure of the friction ridges represent?

5. Compare the location and sequence of red dots with that of your classmates and examine the similarities and differences with the placement of minutiae. Did everyone select the same features in exactly the same places? Why might you observe differences in dot placement?

Part II

Latent Print Development

Chapter 8

Introduction to Processing Methods

Objectives

- Understand physical and chemical processing methods for porous and nonporous substrates
- Explore how environmental factors and deposition time contribute to the persistence of latent prints on various substrates

8.1 Background

Latent prints are invisible friction ridge impressions left on a surface or object by chance. Latent prints must be developed with powders or chemicals to make them visible. Physical processing refers to using dry or aqueous fingerprint powders to develop latent prints. Fingerprint powders are used primarily at crime scenes. The powder particles adhere to the oils and moisture in latent prints when applied with a fingerprint brush. Chemical processing requires chemical reagents and solvents. Chemical reagents react with a variety of components in the latent print matrix, such as lipids, salts, or amino acids.

Some forensic laboratories use only a few different processing methods, while others use numerous processing techniques in particular sequences. Chemical reagents are used in sequence in order to maximize the development of latent prints. Some reagents also may inhibit others and must therefore be utilized in a particular order. For example, when processing a porous item such as a piece of paper, there are several chemicals that can be used to maximize the number of latent prints recovered: indanedione, DFO, ninhydrin, and physical developer. These four reagents must be used in the order listed so as to develop the maximum number of latent prints.

The quality of the latent prints developed with chemical reagents depends on several factors: the condition of the substrate, environmental effects, the type and amount of matrix deposited, and the method of development. The substrate may be porous or nonporous, textured or smooth, curved or flat, clean or dirty. Latent prints are exposed to environmental effects such as rain, wind, humidity, or physical obliteration. The friction ridges depositing the latent print may have excess moisture, lotions, or contaminants or may be nearly dry. The method of development may be sensitive (such as indanedione) or unselective (in the case of granular fingerprint powders).

The two most common substrates are porous and nonporous substrates. Different reagents are used for each type of substrate. Porous surfaces—such as paper, cardboard, or wood—are absorbent. Latent print residues deposited onto porous surfaces are absorbed by the substrate. Nonporous surfaces—such as glass, metal, or plastic—are not absorbent. Latent print residues deposited onto nonporous substrates remain on the surface and are therefore more susceptible to environmental effects and physical obliteration.

Latent print residue is composed mainly of eccrine sweat excreted onto the friction ridges through pores located along the ridges. Eccrine sweat is ~98% water. Latent prints are mostly composed of water; thus, they begin to evaporate as soon as they are deposited. A latent print deposited in a hot, dry environment will evaporate much faster than a latent deposited in a cold or humid environment. Latent prints may also be composed of sebaceous sweat, which is present on nonfriction ridge skin. When an individual touches the face or hair, sebaceous sweat is transferred to the friction ridges and may consequently be deposited as sebaceous latent prints. Specific chemical reagents react with specific components of eccrine or sebaceous sweat.

At this time, it is not possible to accurately age latent prints. If a latent print is recovered from a surface, one cannot determine how long that latent print has persisted on the surface. Various research papers have explored ageing latent prints by analyzing the breakdown of certain components of the eccrine and sebaceous sweat over time. However, there is too much variation between individuals and substrates for these methods to be implemented as yet.

The following exercise explores the concept that latent prints persist on various surfaces based on the type of substrate, environmental factors, and time since deposition. In this laboratory exercise, latent fingerprints will be deposited on various nonporous substrates and left either indoors or in an outdoor environment for various lengths of time. The prints will be developed with fingerprint powder and lifted onto fingerprint cards. The quality of the resulting fingerprints will be compared and contrasted.

8.2 Materials

- Gloves
- Lab coat
- Safety glasses
- Fine-tipped permanent marker
- Thermometer for measuring ambient temperature
- Eight glass items (microscope slides, kitchen glassware, etc.)
- Eight plastic items (disposable plastic plates, cups, etc.)
- Eight aluminum items (soda cans, cyanoacrylate fuming trays, etc.)
- Fingerprint brush
- Black fingerprint powder
- Roll of 2″ latent lift tape
- Eight white latent lift cards

8.3 Exercise

Part I: Persistence of Latent Prints

1. Label four glass items, four plastic items, and four aluminum items with the following information (these four items will be placed in an outdoor environment):
   a. Initials
   b. Date
   c. Weather (sunny, cloudy, rainy, windy, etc.)
   d. Type of environment (parking lot, landscaped area, etc.)
   e. Ambient temperature
   f. Relative humidity
   g. Deposition time (10 min, 30 min, 90 min, and 1+ week)

2. Label four glass items, four plastic items, and four aluminum items with the following information (these four items will be placed in an indoor environment):

   a. Initials

   b. Date

   c. Ambient temperature

   d. Relative humidity

   e. Deposition time (10 min, 30 min, 90 min, and 1+ week)

3. Deposit one latent fingerprint on each item.

4. Immediately place four of each substrate type indoors and four of each substrate type in an outdoor environment.

5. At the times indicated below, process one indoor item of each substrate and one outdoor item of each substrate with black fingerprint powder (as described in steps 6 to 12).

   a. 10 min

   b. 30 min

   c. 90 min

   d. 1+ week

6. Pour out a small amount of black fingerprint powder.

7. Dip the fingerprint brush in the powder and shake or twirl to remove the excess powder.

8. Lightly twirl the fingerprint brush across the surface until friction ridges are visible (Figure 8.1).

9. Peel a length of fingerprint lift tape from the roll and place the end on one side of the developed latent print.

10. Sweep your finger across the tape and press out any bubbles (Figure 8.2).

11. Lift the tape and place it on the white side of a latent lift card. (Figure 8.3)

Figure 8.1
"Dusting" for fingerprints with black fingerprint powder and brush.

Figure 8.2
Latent lift tape is used to lift the developed latent print from the surface.

Figure 8.3
A latent print is transferred with latent lift tape to a latent lift card.

12. Label the latent lift card with the following information:
    a. Initials
    b. Date
    c. Weather (if applicable)
    d. Type of environment (if applicable)
    e. Ambient temperature
    f. Relative humidity
    g. Deposition time (10 min, 30 min, 90 min, and 1+ week)
13. Compare and contrast the quality of the latent lifts from each substrate type, environment type, and deposition time.

8.4 Post-Lab Questions

1. How do fingerprint powders develop fingerprints on nonporous surfaces?

2. What variables contribute to the quality of a latent fingerprint processed with fingerprint powders or chemical reagents?

3. Compare and contrast the developed fingerprints based on substrate type (metal, glass, or plastic). Which latent prints resulted in the best-quality latent lifts? Why?

4. Compare and contrast the developed fingerprints based on time since deposition (10 min, 30 min, 90 min, and 1+ week). Which latent prints resulted in the best-quality latent lifts? Why?

5. Compare and contrast the developed fingerprints based on environment (indoors or outdoors). Which latent prints resulted in the best-quality latent lifts? Why?

Chapter 9

Forensic Light Sources

Objectives

- Understand how light is used as a forensic tool
- Visualize latent prints with oblique white lighting
- Visualize latent prints with a fluorescent light source

9.1 Background

Forensic scientists utilize various wavelengths of light as nondestructive tools for the visualization of latent prints. Any latent print development process should be preceded by a nondestructive visual examination of the item of interest using oblique lighting. Oblique lighting refers to shining a beam of white light at oblique angles to the surface in order to visualize latent prints that cannot readily be seen with ambient light. Oblique lighting allows the forensic scientist to observe three-dimensional details on a surface where light and shadow are created by the light beam. For example, a smartphone screen held at eye level may appear clean, but if that smart phone is tilted in the light, latent prints are revealed on the surface.

Light travels in waves. The distance between the crests of the wave is known as the wavelength, which is measured in nanometers (nm) and is the measure of intensity of that light. Light waves with longer wavelengths have lower energy than light waves with shorter wavelengths. For example, the ultraviolet waves emitted by the sun have a shorter wavelength than colors of the visible spectrum. Prolonged exposure to direct sunlight can result in sunburn.

As light interacts with a substrate, it is absorbed, reflected, and/or transmitted by the surface. The texture and reflectance of the surface determines what color that surface appears to the human eye. The colors humans can see with the naked eye—such as the colors of the rainbow—are in the visible spectrum of electromagnetic radiation. The visible spectrum consists of light with wavelengths between 350 and 750 nm (Figure 9.1). For example, what the human eye sees as green is in fact light waves reflected at 500–550 nm.

Light not only travels in waves but also reacts with surfaces as units of energy known as *photons*. When a photon hits a surface, the molecules that make up that surface absorb the energy and enter an "excited" state. Since atoms always seek their ground (neutral) energy state, the energy is emitted from the molecule (Figure 9.2). Fluorescence is observed when the emitted wavelength is longer than the absorbed wavelength after the light reacts with matter and loses energy. Chemical fingerprint development reagents utilize fluorescence in order to visualize low-contrast latent prints. For example, if a latent print is developed with cyanoacrylate fuming on a white or patterned surface, the white or transparent print will be difficult to visualize and photograph. The print is treated with a fluorescent dye stain in order to make the print "glow" against the background and increase its contrast and visibility. Materials only fluoresce, or glow, when energy is constantly applied to the surface. For example, if a dye stain glows only under green light, it ceases to glow when that green light is removed.

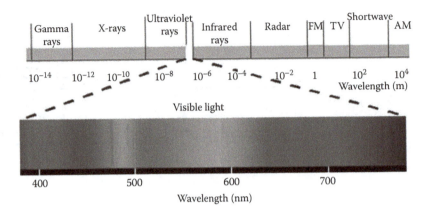

Figure 9.1
The color spectrum (the range of colors visible to the human eye) is a narrow range of wavelengths within the electromagnetic spectrum.

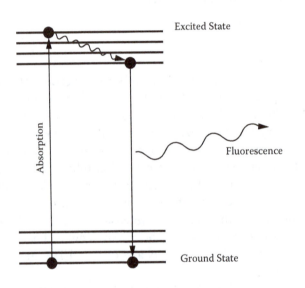

Figure 9.2
Fluorescence is observed when light is absorbed, loses energy as it interacts with matter, and is emitted at a longer wavelength.

Fluorescence must be viewed through barrier filters of specific colors depending on the color of light used to view the fluorescence (Table 9.1). There are a multitude of fluorescent fingerprint reagents and powders used to develop latent prints on nonporous and porous substrates. These reagents will be explored in later sections of this text.

In this lab, an item of evidence will be processed with fluorescent fingerprint powder. The resulting fingerprints, along with various preprocessed items, will be observed with an alternate light source (ALS) or laser.

9.2 Materials

- Gloves
- Lab coat

TABLE 9.1

Wavelengths, Colors of Light, and Associated Barrier Filters and Fluorescent Fingerprint Reagents

Wavelength (nm)	Light Color	Barrier Filter	Fluorescent Fingerprint Reagent/Powder
350–400	UV	UV	Ardrox, Basic Yellow 40, RAM
400–445	Blue	Yellow	Yellow/green fluorescent powder, Acid Yellow 7
445–515	Blue/Green	Orange	Acid Yellow 7, orange fluorescent powder, Rhodamine 6G, MBD, RAM
515–575	Green	Red	RAM, Rhodamine 6G, DFO, Indanedione, red fluorescent fingerprint powder

- Safety glasses
- Flashlight
- Permanent marker
- Nonporous item
- Orange fluorescent fingerprint powder
- Feather duster fingerprint brush
- 2″ latent lift tape
- Black latent lift cards
- Various items processed with fluorescent chemical reagents (such as indanedione, DFO, Rhodamine 6G)
- ALS or laser
- Red, orange, and/or yellow barrier filters or colored safety glasses

9.3 Exercises

Part I: Fluorescent Fingerprint Powder

1. Deposit one latent print onto one nonporous item (a plastic plate, cup, aluminum can, etc.)
2. Examine the item with oblique lighting by shining the light at various oblique angles to examine the surface for latent prints. Circle visible prints with a permanent marker.
3. Dip the tip of a feather duster fingerprint brush in orange fluorescent fingerprint powder. Gently shake off the excess.
4. Pass the fingerprint brush over the surface of the item several times.
5. Lift the resulting latent print with 2″ latent lift tape onto a black latent lift card.

Part II: Observing Fluorescence

1. Observe the latent lift card from Part I under green light with an orange/red barrier filter or red protective glasses.
2. Observe various items of different substrates processed with fluorescent chemical reagents using proper colored glasses for each spectrum of light (Table 9.1).
3. Record your observations in Figure 9.3.

Item Description	Process	Wavelength (nm)	Color of Light	Colored Filter
Example – Soda can	Rhodamine 6G	525 nm	Green	Red

Figure 9.3
Part II: Observing fluorescence—record your observations.

9.4 Post-Lab Questions

1. What is oblique lighting?
2. Light travels in _____ and acts on matter as a unit of energy called a _____.
3. What is fluorescence?
4. What colored light and barrier filter are required to view a latent print developed with orange fluorescent fingerprint powder?
5. Which color light and barrier filter (or safety glasses) are used in conjunction with the following chemical reagents?
   a. Rhodamine 6G
   b. Ardrox
   c. Indanedione
   d. DFO

Chapter 10

Physical Processing Methods

Objectives

- Understand the various physical processing methods for developing latent prints
- Develop latent prints on nonporous substrates using physical processing methods

10.1 Background

The most commonly recognized latent print development technique is black fingerprint powder. Powder processing comprises the application of black fingerprint powder to a surface with a specific type of fingerprint brush. Black powder processing is best utilized at crime scenes on static items such as stair rails, windows, and doorframes. This is colloquially referred to as "dusting" a scene. Portable items of evidence should always be collected for processing at a forensic laboratory, since a forensic laboratory is a controlled environment and is the appropriate place to develop latent prints using a sequential series of chemical reagents. Chemical reagents are more selective and thus more efficacious.

Powder processing is considered a physical processing method rather than a chemical reaction. Powder granules adhere to the wet and oily components of latent print residues when the fingerprint powder is applied with an applicator such as a fingerprint brush. Powders are a low-cost and efficient method for developing fingerprints on nonporous substrates.

There are six types of fingerprint powder, each available in a variety of colors: granular fingerprint powder, magnetic powder, fluorescent powder, metallic flake powder, nanopowder, and infrared powder. (Nanopowders and infrared powders are fairly new products that are not widely used.) The color of powder chosen should contrast with the surface of interest so the latent prints are clearly visible when they develop. For example, black fingerprint powder is used on light-colored surfaces. Dark-colored surfaces are processed with white, gray, silver, or bi-chromatic fingerprint powder. Bi-chromatic powder, also known as dual contrast powder, is a blend of black and aluminum powders. The aluminum particles adhere to latent print residues and stand out on dark backgrounds while the dark-colored particles provide contrast on light-colored items. The developed latent prints are lifted onto white latent lift cards.

Magnetic powder is a blend of granular fingerprint powder and magnetic metallic particles. The magnetic particles carry the fingerprint powder, which attaches to the magnet-tipped applicator in a bundle that acts as a brush (Figure 10.1). This "brush" is gently passed over a surface to develop latent fingerprints. Magnetic powder is advantageous because it is a more sensitive technique, it results in prints with less background noise, it can be used on greasy or dirty surfaces, it is successful on difficult surfaces such as Styrofoam™, and it is easy to clean because loose particles can be reclaimed with the magnetic wand applicator. Regardless of the advantages of magnetic powder, it cannot be used on vertical surfaces, large areas, or ferric (iron-containing) metal surfaces.

There are a variety of powder applicators specific to each type of fingerprint powder. Traditional powders are applied with a fiberglass fingerprint brush. Magnetic powders are applied with magnet tipped applicators known as "magna brushes" or wands. Fluorescent powders are applied with feather duster fingerprint brushes.

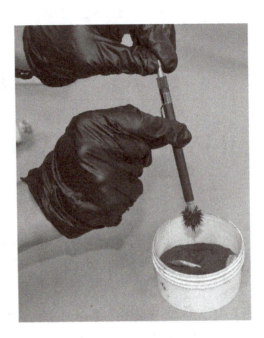

Figure 10.1
Magnetic powder contains magnetic particles that carry the fingerprint powder on a magnet-tipped applicator in a bundle that acts as a brush.

Figure 10.2
Mikrosil™ Casting Putty is a common silicone casting material used to lift powdered fingerprints from curved or textured surfaces.

Latent prints developed with fingerprint powder should first be documented in situ with photography, then lifted with adhesive material such as fingerprint lifting tape or silicone rubber casting material. Fingerprints lifted from a surface are adhered to a latent lift card where the case information, sketch of the location, and directionality of the print are recorded. While latent lift tape is the most common method for lifting a powdered print from a surface, it is not suitable for lifting latent prints from curved or rough surfaces. Silicone rubber casting material is often used to lift prints from curved or textured surfaces. It consists of a soft casting material and a catalyst, which initiates a chemical reaction that hardens the material. The casting material is combined with a catalyst and applied over a latent print developed with fingerprint powder. After a few minutes, it hardens to a rubbery cast. The cast is removed with the powdered print embedded in the surface (Figure 10.2).

In this laboratory exercise, latent prints are developed on a variety of surfaces using granular and magnetic fingerprint powders and lifted with tape and silicone casting material.

10.2 Materials

- Pen
- Gloves
- Lab coat
- Safety glasses
- One dark-colored nonporous item
- One light-colored nonporous item
- Black fingerprint powder
- Bi-chromatic fingerprint powder
- Fiberglass fingerprint brush
- White latent lift cards
- 2″ latent lift tape
- Styrofoam™ cup
- One nonporous item with a curved, rough, or smooth surface
- Black magnetic fingerprint powder
- Magnetic fingerprint powder applicator
- Mikrosil™ Casting material (or other forensic silicone casting material)
- Wooden stick or plastic spoon for mixing the putty with the catalyst

10.3 Exercises

Part I: Black and Bi-Chromatic Fingerprint Powders

1. Deposit latent prints onto a light-colored nonporous item.
2. Visually inspect the surface of the item with oblique white light.
3. Apply a light layer of black powder onto a fiberglass fingerprint brush and shake off the excess.
4. Lightly pass the brush over the surface until friction ridges are visible.
5. Lift the developed latent prints onto a white latent lift card using latent lift tape.
6. Fill out mock case information, complete a sketch, and note the "up" direction of the print as shown in Figure 10.3.
7. Repeat steps 2–6 with bi-chromatic fingerprint powder on a dark-colored nonporous surface.

Part II: Magnetic Fingerprint Powder and Casting Material

1. Deposit latent prints on the Styrofoam™ cup and the surface of a second curved, rough, or smooth nonporous item.
2. Visually inspect the surface of the item with oblique white light.
3. Dip the magnetic end of the magnetic applicator into the black magnetic fingerprint powder (Figure 10.3).
4. Gently pass the powder "brush" over the surface until friction ridges develop.

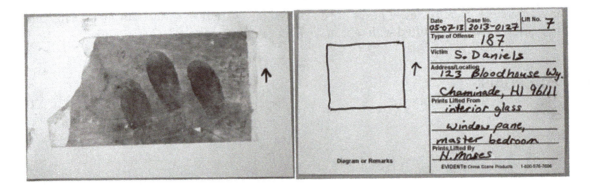

Figure 10.3
The front and back of a latent lift card with completed, thorough documentation.

Figure 10.4
Pulling up the opposing end of the magna brush retracts the magnet in the magna brush and releases the magnetic fingerprint powder.

5. Release the excess fingerprint powder back into the jar by lifting up the rod on the top of the applicator (Figure 10.4).

6. Squeeze ~3″ of white Mikrosil™ or other forensic silicone casting material onto the shiny side of a white latent lift card (Figure 10.5).

7. Squeeze 3″ of blue Mikrosil™ catalyst ("hardener") next to the casting putty and mix the two together until the mixture appears white. (If using another forensic silicone casting material, follow the directions provided with the packaging.)

8. Gently apply a thick layer of the silicone casting mixture over the powdered latent prints.

9. Allow the material to harden for 5–10 min.

10. Peel the material from the surface.

11. Repeat steps 2–10 with the Styrofoam™ cup.

Part II: DFO

DFO Working Solution

0.25 g DFO
40 ml methanol
20 ml acetic acid
DFO working solution
60 ml DFO stock solution
940 ml HFE 7100

1. Prepare the DFO stock solution by dissolving the DFO in methanol and acetic acid in a 75–150 ml glass beaker over a magnetic stirrer for approximately 20 min until completely dissolved.
2. In a 1 l glass beaker, slowly add the HFE 7100 solvent to the stock solution and stir until combined.
3. Dip or spray the white paper from Part I with the DFO working solution until the item is saturated.
4. Hang the item to dry in a fume hood.
5. When dry, heat the item in an incubator at 100°C for 20 min.
6. View the item with a red barrier filter or red safety glasses under green light (530–570 nm) using an alternate light source or laser.
7. Circle any new fingerprints with a blue pen.

Part III: Ninhydrin

Ninhydrin Working Solution

2.5 g ninhydrin crystals
23 ml ethanol
1 ml ethyl acetate
2.5 ml acetic acid
500 ml HFE 7100

1. Dissolve the ninhydrin crystals in ethanol, ethyl acetate, and acetic acid in a 750 ml–1 l beaker over a magnetic stirrer.
2. When the ninhydrin is completely dissolved, slowly add the HFE 7100 solvent.
3. Dip or spray the white paper from Part II with the ninhydrin working solution until the item is saturated.
4. Hang the item to dry in a fume hood.
5. Take note of any fingerprints developed with the ninhydrin that were not previously developed with indanedione and/or DFO.

11.4 Post-Lab Questions

1. What makes a substrate porous?
2. How do latent print residues adhere to porous substrates?
3. Why must the chemical reagents be used in a particular sequence? What is the proper sequence for processing latent prints on porous substrates?

4. Which chemical reagent—indanedione, DFO, or ninhydrin—resulted in the most fingerprints? Which chemical reagent resulted in the best-quality fingerprints?

5. If it were necessary to choose only one of the reagents listed above, which would you choose and why?

References

1. Almog, J. et al. 1999. Latent fingerprint visualization by 1,2-indanedione and related compounds: Preliminary results. *J. Forensic Sci.* 44(1): 114–118.
2. Wiesner, S. et al. 2001. Chemical development of latent fingerprints: 1,2-Indanedione has come of age. *J. Forensic Sci.* 46(5): 1082–1084.
3. Wallace-Kunkel, C. et al. 2007. Optimisation and evaluation of 1,2-Indanedione for use as a fingermark reagent and its application to real samples. *Forensic Sci. Int.* 168(1): 14–26.
4. Bicknell, D.E. and Ramotowski, R.S. 2008. Use of an optimized 1,2-indanedione process for the development of latent prints. *J. Forensic Sci.* 53(5): 1108–1116.
5. Azoury, M., Zamir, A., Oz, C. and Wiesner, S. 2002. The effect of 1,2-Indanedione, a latent fingerprint reagent on subsequent DNA profiling. *J. Forensic Sci.* 47(3): 586–588.

Chapter **12**

Chemical Processing Methods
Nonporous Substrates

Objectives

- Describe and give examples of nonporous substrates
- Understand how latent print residues adhere to nonporous substrates
- Recognize the various chemical reagents and processes used to develop latent prints on nonporous substrates

12.1 Background

Nonporous substrates such as metal, glass, or plastic are impermeable to gases and liquids. They do not absorb latent print residues as porous substrates do. Instead, latent prints sit on the surface of a nonporous item and are therefore especially vulnerable to environmental effects such as wind, rain, temperature, and humidity. As with porous substrates, a majority of the water component of eccrine sweat evaporates over time. Because the latent prints remain on the surface, nonporous items should be handled with great care. Evidentiary items should be handled in heavily textured or rough surfaces or on the edges of the item so as not to rub off any latents on the smooth surfaces.

Cyanoacrylate fuming (known colloquially as Super Glue® fuming) both makes latents visible to the naked eye and adheres latents to a substrate, making them more durable. After a visual examination and/or alternate light source examination, cyanoacrylate fuming is most often the first step when processing non-porous items of evidence. The process involves placing an evidentiary item in an enclosed chamber (fuming chamber). Liquid cyanoacrylate in the chamber is heated until it vaporizes (turns into a gas). The cyano-acrylate vapors adhere to the latent print residues and build up like building blocks (monomers) to form a stable polymer or chain of molecules. This process, called *polymerization*, is accelerated by the addition of humidity to the chamber. The resulting fingerprint is transparent or white in color (Figure 12.1).

Cyanoacrylate fuming is often performed in a commercial fuming chamber (Figure 12.2). If a commer-cial chamber is not available, a fuming chamber can be constructed from any enclosed container such as a fish tank with an airtight lid, large Tupperware® container, or cardboard box (Figure 12.3). Several drops of cyanoacrylate are poured onto an aluminum tray or a piece of aluminum foil. The foil is placed on a low-level heat source such as a mug warmer or light bulb. (A kitchen hot plate is unadvisable as it may cause a fire in the chamber.) A cup of boiling water is placed in the chamber to produce steam in order to facilitate the polymerization reaction. A "test print" is placed in the fuming chamber along with the evidentiary items in order to gauge whether the evidence is fumed properly during development. The process is complete when the test print appears to have a light layer of white residue deposited along the friction ridges.

During the polymerization reaction, layers of cyanoacrylate material build up on the latent print resi-dues to form a three-dimensional print. They are therefore best viewed and photographed with oblique light-ing. When light is held at an oblique angle to the surface, light and shadow allow the analyst to see more

Figure 12.1
A latent print on a DVD processed with cyanoacrylate fuming.

Figure 12.2
Processing an AK-47 type rifle in a cyanoacrylate fuming chamber.

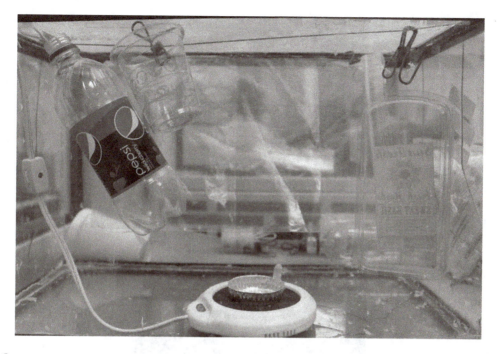

Figure 12.3
An improvised cyanoacrylate fuming chamber.

detail than with ambient light. With cyanoacrylate fuming, it is often possible to see minute details along the friction ridges such as pores and edge shapes.

Regardless of the background color of the substrate, cyanoacrylate-developed prints are often difficult to observe and document, as they are frequently transparent or white in color. Subsequent processes are necessary to enhance the contrast of cyanoacrylate prints. Fluorescent dye stains selectively adhere to the cyanoacrylate polymer. There are a wide variety of dye stains that fluoresce under various wavelengths (colors) of light. Some of the most common dye stains are Ardrox, basic yellow 40, and Rhodamine 6G.

Ardrox fluoresces under long-wave UV radiation with a yellow barrier filter. Basic yellow 40 fluoresces under both long-wave UV radiation and blue-green light with yellow or orange barrier filters. Rhodamine 6G is perhaps the most popular cyanoacrylate dye stain utilized in the United States (Figure 12.4). It fluoresces under green light with orange and red barrier filters (depending on the alternate light source's wavelength). A barrier filter is used to view fluorescent prints with the naked eye by allowing a certain range of wavelengths of light to pass through to the eye while the filter blocks the rest of the light. Colored safety glasses, camera filters, or Plexiglas® sheets are types of barrier filters. Cyanoacrylate-fumed items are dipped or sprayed with a dye stain, rinsed, and allowed to air dry. The items are then viewed under an alternate light source or laser with the appropriate barrier filters.

Several cyanoacrylate complexes have been developed that are mixtures of aqueous cyanoacrylate and a dye stain. These complexes are one-step reagents that dye stain friction ridges as the polymerization reaction occurs. One of these dye complexes, Lumicyano™, has been as successful as an alternative to cyanoacrylate fuming and staining with Rhodamine 6G.[1] The one-step process proceeds in the same manner as the two-step process outlined above. The aqueous cyanoacrylate-dye complex is placed on a tray over a heat source, and the vaporized complex both fumes and dyes the friction ridges of latent prints.

Vacuum metal deposition (VMD) is another recommended process for developing latent prints on nonporous items though it has also been successful with porous and semiporous items. Evidentiary items are placed in a VMD chamber and the air is evacuated to create a vacuum. Small amounts of metals are vaporized. The vaporized metals adhere to the substrate everywhere except latent prints. It is especially useful

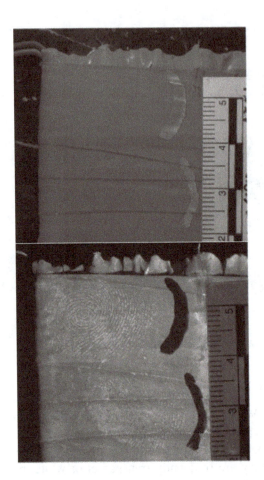

Figure 12.4
Latent prints on a nonporous surface developed with cyanoacrylate fuming (top) and Rhodamine 6G dye staining (bottom).

for difficult substrates (such as fabric), substrates containing latent prints older than two years, or as a final resort when all other techniques have failed.

Semiporous items are a special case of mixed substrates. They have properties of both porous and nonporous items and are thus processed with both porous and nonporous chemical reagents. The suggested processing sequence for a semiporous item is cyanoacrylate fuming, indanedione, DFO, ninhydrin, and cyanoacrylate dye staining.

In this laboratory exercise, latent prints will be developed on a nonporous item using cyanoacrylate fuming and dye staining.

12.2 Materials

- Gloves
- Lab coat
- Safety glasses
- Black permanent marker
- Red wax pencil
- Magnifying glass or fingerprint loop

- One nonporous item
- Flashlight
- Fuming chamber (or large plastic box with a tight-fitting lid and a mug warmer)
- Cyanoacrylate ester (or store-bought superglue®)
- Cyanoacrylate fuming tray (or aluminum foil folded into a boat or tray shape)
- Test print substrate (such as a square of aluminum foil)
- Cup of boiling water (if the fuming chamber does not have a built-in humidifier)
- Two 500 ml wash bottles
- 1 l glass beaker
- Magnetic stirrer or glass rod
- Rhodamine 6G powder
- Methanol or distilled water
- ALS or laser
- Orange/Red barrier filters or glasses

12.3 Exercises

Part I: Cyanoacrylate Fuming

1. Deposit several fingerprints on a nonporous item and on the test print substrate.
2. Place a fuming chamber in a fume hood.
3. Place a heat source inside the fuming chamber.
4. Place the aluminum foil or tray onto the heat source.
5. Place or hang the item in the fuming chamber so all of the surfaces of the item are exposed to the cyanoacrylate fumes.
6. Plug in the heat source.
7. Place a cup of steaming hot or boiling water into the chamber.
8. Squeeze a dime-sized amount of cyanoacrylate onto the aluminum foil or tray.
9. Seal the chamber.
10. Allow the items to fume until a light layer of white residue is visible on the test print. (Do not overprocess! Superglue will build up in the furrows between the ridges and cannot be removed.)
11. Turn off the heat source, open the chamber, remove the glue, and allow the fumes to vent in the fume hood.
12. Remove the item from the chamber.
13. Examine the item with oblique lighting under magnification.
14. Circle any visible prints with a red wax pencil.

Part II: Dye Staining

Rhodamine 6G Working Solution

0.025 g Rhodamine 6G (R6G) powder

1 l Methanol or distilled water

1. Dissolve the R6G in 500 ml methanol or water in a 750–1000 ml glass beaker over a magnetic stirrer or stir thoroughly with a glass rod.

2. Transfer the R6G working solution to a 500 ml wash bottle or spray bottle.

3. Fill another 500 ml wash bottle or spray bottle with the remaining 500 ml methanol or water.

4. Spray the entire cyanoacrylate-fumed nonporous item from Part I with the R6G working solution.

5. Gently rinse the item with methanol or water (depending on the carrier solvent used).

6. Dry the item in a fume hood.

7. Observe the fluorescence under green illumination (515–550 nm) using red goggles.

8. Circle any new fingerprints with a black permanent marker.

12.4 Post-Lab Questions

1. What makes a substrate nonporous?

2. What are six components of the cyanoacrylate fuming process?

3. Observe the fingerprints from part I of this laboratory exercise under magnification. Describe in detail the appearance of the cyanoacrylate-fumed prints.

4. List three fluorescent cyanoacrylate dye stains. Indicate the wavelength(s)/color light(s) used to view the resulting latent prints and the color barrier filter(s) necessary to view the reaction product.

5. Compare and contrast the results of cyanoacrylate fuming with the results of the subsequent dye staining.

Reference

1. Prete, C., Galmiche, L., Quenum-Possy-Berry, F. G., Allain, C., Thiburce, N. and Colard, T.2013. Lumicyano™: A new fluorescent cyanoacrylate for a one-step luminescent latent fingermark development. *Forensic Sci. Int.* 233:104–112.

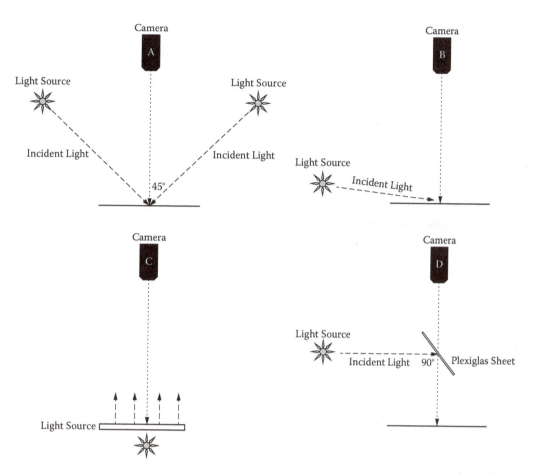

Figure 14.3

A schematic diagram demonstrating the direct lighting photographic technique (top left), the oblique lighting photographic technique (top right), the back lighting photographic technique (bottom left), and the front directional lighting technique (bottom right).

Figure 14.4 Various camera filters for photographing fluorescent latent prints under an alternate light source or laser.

Contemporaneous notes, forms, worksheets, and photographs are used to write a final report. A final report is a detailed narrative of all forensic analyses. It is an objective, organized, thorough, clear, and concise report of the fingerprint analyst's actions, observations, and results. The final report should be written so all individuals involved with a case (investigators, attorneys, jurors, etc.) can understand the details of the case, the actions taken, and the forensic analyses performed.

In this laboratory exercise, latent prints will be developed on one porous item (utilizing ninhydrin) and one nonporous item (utilizing cyanoacrylate fuming). The processes will be documented with contemporaneous notes, photographs, and a final report.

14.2 Materials

- Gloves
- Lab coat
- Safety glasses
- Digital SLR camera with a standard lens and macro lens
- Note paper
- Pen
- Index cards
- Scale (ruler or tape measure)
- One porous item with latent prints
- One nonporous item with latent prints
- Ninhydrin
- Cyanoacrylate fuming chamber
- Cyanoacrylate
- Camera stand with mounted lights
- Flashlight
- Computer
- Printer

14.3 Exercises

Part I: Documentation of Evidence

1. Begin contemporaneous notes by recording the date and time of receipt of the evidentiary items and the mock case information as provided by your instructor.
2. Note the case information and item number for each evidentiary item on index cards.
3. Using a digital SLR camera fitted with a standard lens, photograph each item of evidence with a scale and identification card (index card).

Part II: Documentation of Latent Prints

1. Record your actions and observations throughout Part II by taking detailed notes of the following:
   a. Processes performed
   b. The outcome of each process (number of latent prints developed and other observations)
   c. Type of camera, camera settings, and the photographic lighting technique used to capture each latent print.
2. Process the porous item of evidence with ninhydrin (see Lab 11, Part III).
3. Photograph visible friction ridge detail using the direct lighting method.
   a. Place the item on a copy stand.
   b. Illuminate the item with two lights mounted to the copy stand and tilted at 45-degree angle to the base of the copy stand.

c. Place a sticky scale on the evidence close to, but not overlapping, the friction ridges of interest. The sticky scale should be labeled with the case number, item number, arbitrary latent print identifier (e.g., "Latent #1" or "L001"), and initials.

d. Adjust the lens of the camera to zoom in on the friction ridges of interest so the ridges and scale fill the frame of the view finder.

e. Using either manual or auto focus, photograph the item.

4. Process the nonporous item of evidence with cyanoacrylate fuming (see Lab 12, Part I).

5. Photograph visible friction ridge detail using the oblique lighting method.
   a. Place the item on a copy stand.

   b. Place a sticky scale on the evidence close to, but not overlapping, the friction ridges of interest. The sticky scale should be labeled with the case number, item number, latent print identifier, and initials.

   c. Adjust the lens of the camera to zoom in on the friction ridges of interest so the ridges and scale fill the frame of the view finder.

   d. Hold a flashlight at an oblique angle to the friction ridges of interest and adjust the angle until the cyanoacrylate-fumed ridges are visible.

   e. Using either manual or auto focus, photograph the item.

   f. Take several photographs with the flashlight held at various oblique angles.

Part III: Final Report

1. Upload all photographs from Part I and Part II to a computer.

2. Prepare a narrative final report based on your contemporaneous notes and photographs.

14.4 Post-Lab Questions

1. List five types of documentation used by fingerprint analysts.

2. Name and describe the four most common photographic lighting techniques.

3. List the photographic lighting techniques used to record latent prints developed with the following chemical and physical processes.
   a. Ninhydrin
   b. Fingerprint powder
   c. Indanedione
   d. Cyanoacrylate fuming

4. Why is oblique lighting the most efficacious lighting technique for latent prints developed with the cyanoacrylate fuming method?

5. What is the purpose of the final report?

Crime Scene Processing

Objectives

- Learn how the presence, directionality, and location of latent prints at a crime scene contribute to an investigation
- Process a vehicle scene with fingerprint powders and document the resulting latent lifts
- Process and analyze the point of entry (POE) of a residential burglary scene

15.1 Background

Processing evidence (items associated with a crime scene that may determine guilt or innocence in a court of law) and crime scenes (locations where crimes takes place) involves both forensic knowledge and analytical skills. The skilled crime scene investigator analyzes not only the presence of latent prints and other forensic evidence but also the significance of that evidence, which may be elucidated by the context of that print. Context is the latent print's location and directionality on an item or surface. The POE of a crime scene is often the most productive region for latent prints. This is because gaining entry into a residence or vehicle often involves force and physical action such as manipulating doors and windows or climbing into the scene. Latent prints in these areas can prove intent.

Three of the most common crime scenes are vehicle scenes, residential scenes, and commercial scenes. Vehicles are used as weapons in hit-and-runs, as transport for criminals, as transport for contraband, and as the target of theft. Latent prints on the exterior of a vehicle are insufficient to prove criminal intent, as vehicles parked in public areas may be touched by anyone passing by the vehicle. Most surfaces inside a vehicle are textured or frequently handled and are thus poor surfaces for latent print recovery. The most successful areas for recovering latent prints are windows, doorframes, rearview mirrors, and personal items located inside the vehicle.

The most common residential crime is burglary, which is the illegal entry into a building or vehicle, with the intent to commit larceny or other crimes. The most productive place to search for latent prints is the POE, especially a window. A door may be kicked open, forced open with a pry bar or other tool, or opened via the doorknob. Doorknobs are frequently handled and often dirty and therefore an unlikely surface to sustain a latent print of value. Latent prints may also be found in areas that have been disturbed (Figure 15.1).

If the POE is a window, and the glass has not been broken, perform an initial visual examination of the window with oblique lighting and note any visible friction ridge detail by circling it on the glass with a permanent marker or grease pencil. Label each circled area with a unique alphanumeric latent identifier. Process the window for latent prints with black fingerprint powder and lift the prints onto latent lift cards, diagramming the locations and directionality of the latent prints with sketches and arrows (Figure 15.2). Any latent prints corresponding to the circles on the window are labeled with the unique identifier designated on the window. All latent lift cards are numbered or lettered sequentially. A latent print on the exterior of a window does not necessarily indicate criminal intent, just as a latent print on a vehicle does not indicate criminal intent. Also, because it is not yet possible to age a latent print, the print could have been present on

Figure 15.1
Typical ransacked dresser in the master bedroom of a burglary scene offering multiple surfaces for a latent print search.

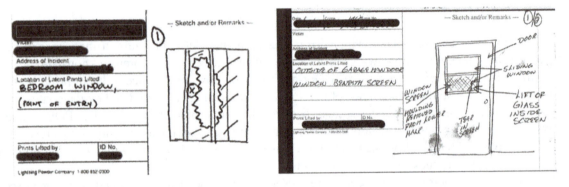

Figure 15.2
The backs of two latent lift cards with associated latent print designations and sketches.

the window for days, weeks, or even years. A print on the inside of the glass pane or window frame, however, can establish not only identity but also intent.

Broken windows provide incriminating evidence in the form of the locations and directionality of latent prints on broken glass pieces and surrounding areas. When a burglar breaks a window, the burglar will often remove glass fragments from the molding of the window frame in order to avoid injury when gaining entry to the residence (Figure 15.3). These fragments, characterized by straight edges on the side originally secured in the molding of the window, often have a thumbprint on one side and an index and/or middle finger on the other. Several pieces of information can be devised from the presence, location, and directionality of these prints: the time of deposit, identity, as well as proof of entry and intent.

In this laboratory exercise, a mock vehicle scene and the POE of a residential burglary scene will be processed for latent prints.

15.2 Materials

- Gloves
- Lab coat

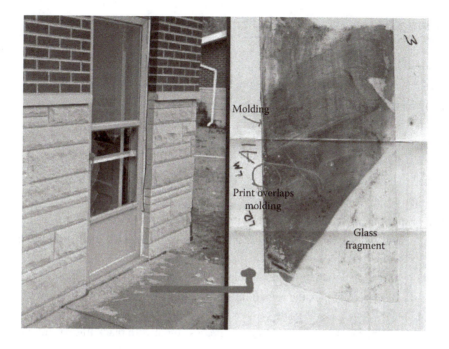

Figure 15.3
Latent prints (right) lifted from glass fragments picked out of the molding (left) of a window.

- Safety glasses
- Flashlight
- Vehicle with latent prints on the exterior
- Black or bi-chromatic fingerprint powder (depending on the color of the vehicle exterior)
- Fiberglass fingerprint brush
- White latent lift cards
- 2″ and/or 4″ latent lift tape
- Window frame with glazing (or glass in a heavy-duty picture frame)
- Easel on which to stand the window
- Black and red permanent markers
- Rock or tool to break the window
- Kraft paper beneath and surrounding the window
- Digital camera

15.3 Exercises

Part I: Vehicle Scene

1. Visually inspect the surface of the vehicle with oblique white light.
2. Process the vehicle exterior with black or bi-chromatic fingerprint powder (see Lab 10, Part I).
3. Lift any developed latent prints onto white latent lift cards with 2″ or 4″ latent lift tape.
4. For each latent print lifted, fill out all mock case information, complete a sketch, and note the directionality of the latent print.

Part II: Residential Burglary—Point of Entry

1. Place the window on an easel over Kraft paper.

2. With the glass intact, push on the glass as if trying to open the window.

3. Examine the glass with oblique lighting.

4. Circle areas of visible friction ridge detail with a red permanent marker and label them numerically or alphabetically.

5. Draw arrows to indicate the "up" direction.

6. Photograph the window to show the locations and directionality of friction ridge detail.

7. Process the window with black fingerprint powder.

8. Lift the latent prints onto white latent lift cards with latent lift tape.

9. For each latent print lifted, fill out all mock case information, complete a sketch, and note the directionality of the prints.

10. Break the glass by throwing a rock through it or hitting the center of it with a tool.

11. With gloveless hands, carefully pick the remaining glass out of the molding of the window frame and drop the fragments onto the floor.

12. Identify the fragments picked from the molding and process them with black fingerprint powder.

13. Lift the developed latent prints onto white latent lift cards using latent lift tape.

14. For each latent print lifted, fill out all mock case information, complete a sketch, and note the directionality of the prints.

15. With all possible pieces of glass removed from the window, demonstrate how someone would place both hands inside the window in an effort to climb into a residence through the window frame.

16. Process the inside of the window frame with black fingerprint powder.

17. Circle visible friction ridge detail with a red permanent marker and label them numerically or alphabetically.

18. Draw arrows to indicate the "up" direction.

19. Photograph the window to show the locations and directionality of friction ridge detail.

20. Lift the latent prints onto white latent lift cards with latent lift tape.

21. For each latent print lifted, fill out all mock case information, complete a sketch, and note the directionality of the print.

15.4 Post-Lab Questions

1. Why might latent prints developed on the exterior of a vehicle be insufficient to support a prosecution?

2. What is the significance of fingerprints found on glass fragments pulled from a window frame at the POE to a residential burglary scene?

3. Compare and contrast latent fingerprints lifted from an intact window to those found on glass fragments removed from the frame of a broken window at a POE to a residential burglary scene.

4. How might the height of the window off the ground affect the position of hands, and, therefore, the directionality and location of latent prints, on a window frame? Would the latent prints be in this same position if the person had climbed out of the window instead of in?

5. What were some of the unexpected challenges that arose while processing the vehicle and the window?

Chapter **16**

Fingerprint Comparisons
ACE-V Methodology

Objectives

- Understand ACE-V methodology
- Understand the three possible conclusions of a fingerprint comparison
- Practice comparing latent prints to exemplar prints

16.1 Background

The purpose of comparing friction ridge impressions is to determine whether an unknown print and a known print likely originated from the same source. Identifying an individual as the source of a latent print is possible because friction ridge impressions are unique and persistent. Latent prints are developed with fingerprint powders and chemical reagents. Known prints are recorded in ink, powder, or digitally. Comparing latent prints to known prints involves discerning similarities and differences in patterns. The appearance of a latent print depends on the processing method, deposition pressure, distortion, substrate characteristics, the amount and type of matrix on the friction ridges, and the elasticity of the skin.

Exemplar prints are also compared in order to determine an individual's identity or whether he or she has a criminal record. Tenprint examiners compare exemplars with other exemplars. Latent print examiners compare latent prints to exemplars. Regardless of the goal of the comparison, the process is the same. Both processes utilize a methodology known as ACE-V. This methodology standardizes the process of comparing one friction ridge impression to another. There are three possible conclusions to a latent print comparison: exclusion, identification, or inconclusive. The examiner's conclusion is based on a quantitative (numbers, types, and relative positions of minutiae) and qualitative (the quality of the latent, the ridge flow, and other observable features) analysis of the friction ridge impressions.

The latent print examiner compares various features of the latent with the known print in order to come to a conclusion about its possible source (Figure 16.1). Level one detail refers to the overall flow of the ridges, pattern type, and the position of the core and delta (or other observable structural features). Level one detail narrows down the potential source of the print but cannot be used for a conclusive identification. It can, however, lead to an exclusion. If the latent print is a whorl, for example, but the suspect's fingers all display loops, the suspect can be excluded as the source of the latent print.

Level two detail refers to the types and relative positions of minutiae within the pattern. Level two detail is used to identify the possible source of a print. Level three detail refers to the minute features of each friction ridge: edge shapes and the sizes, shapes, and locations of pores. An examination of level three detail can be used to augment an identification. All of the features mentioned above may be utilized when performing ACE-V methodology.

Figure 16.1
A double-loop whorl fingerprint with edge shapes and pores demonstrating level one, two, and three detail.

ACE-V stands for analysis, comparison, evaluation, and verification. In the analysis phase of ACE-V, the overall ridge flow, quality, features, level one and level two detail of the latent print are analyzed. If the comparison is performed on a computer screen, the minutiae can be marked either with red dots or with a color coding scheme that denotes levels of confidence in each minutiae point. One such method, known as GYRO, utilizes four different colors of dots to mark minutiae: green, yellow, red, and orange.[1] This method allows for more transparent documentation and limits the potential for bias. Green dots indicate minutiae of high confidence. Yellow dots indicate minutiae that are less clear. Red dots indicate unclear or questionable minutiae. Orange dots are added during the comparison phase of ACE-V to indicate minutiae that were not initially observed during the analysis phase but were seen after the exemplar was placed next to the unknown print. Regardless of the method used, documentation is important throughout the ACE-V process.

In the comparison phase of ACE-V, the latent and known prints are examined side by side under magnification or on a computer screen. When comparing prints manually, fingerprint pointers—implements resembling pens with pointed tips—are used as "placeholders" as the latent print examiner compares the type and relative position of each minutia point (Figure 16.2). When the examiner is confident that he or she has observed enough detail in the prints to make a final determination, he or she moves on to the evaluation phase.

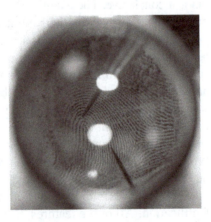

Figure 16.2
A loop fingerprint viewed through a magnifier. Pointers act as "place holders" when examining prints under magnification.

In the evaluation phase of ACE-V, a conclusion is reached as to the likely source of the latent print. As was mentioned above, the conclusion may be an identification, exclusion, or inconclusive. An identification conclusion indicates that the latent print and the known print likely originated from the same source (Figure 16.3). All features must be in agreement. If discrepancies are observed, they must be explainable: for example, due to distortion. An exclusion conclusion indicates that one or more unexplainable dissimilarities exist between the latent and the known print. If neither an identification nor an exclusion can be determined, the result is inconclusive. An inconclusive conclusion is reached if there is not enough detail in the latent print to make an identification or exclusion decision or if the known print is not sufficient to come to a determination.

The verification stage of ACEV is a form of peer review. In the case of nonblind verification, a second competent examiner looks at the first examiner's results and then conducts his or her own ACE process to come to a decision about the source of the unknown print. The preferable method of verification is known as blind verification. In this case, a second latent print examiner performs a completely independent ACE analysis of the latent and known prints and either supports or refutes the initial examiner's conclusions. The second examiner is unaware of the first examiner's conclusions and therefore cannot be biased by that examiner's initial opinion. The drawback of blind verification is that it is time consuming, since each case is examined independently on two separate occasions. While many agencies only employ verification for identification conclusions, research has shown that the erroneous exclusion rate is considerably higher than the erroneous identification rate.[2,3] It is recommended that verification be implemented for all conclusions, not just identifications, for this reason.

In this laboratory exercise, pattern recognition exercises and fingerprint comparisons will be performed using ACE-V methodology.

16.2 Materials

- Pen or pencil
- Figure 16.4
- Figure 16.5
- Figure 16.6
- Figure 16.7

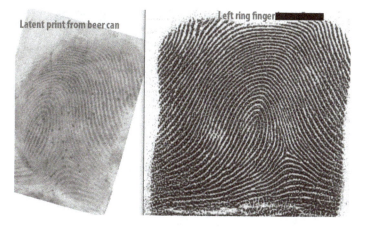

Latent print from beer can

Left ring finger

Figure 16.3

The image on the left is a latent print lifted from a beer bottle collected at a crime scene. The image on the right is the left ring finger of the suspect. The latent fingerprint (left) and the known fingerprint (right) likely originated from the same source.

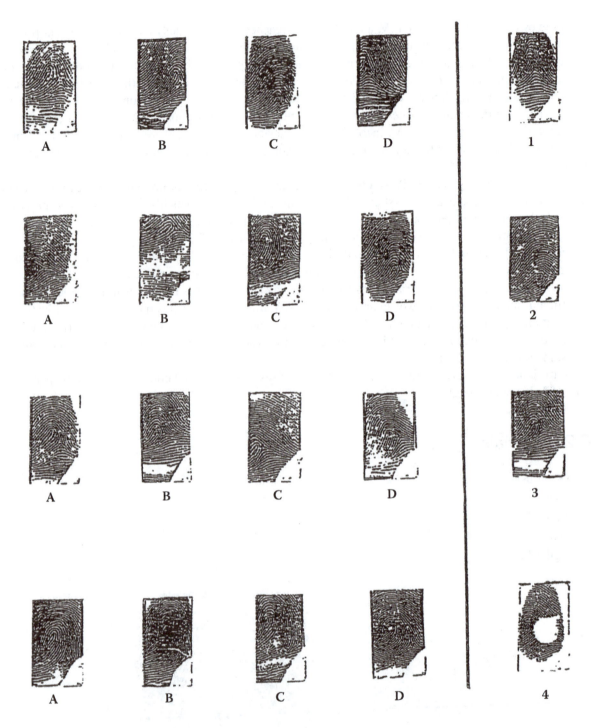

Figure 16.4
Part I: Fingerprint matching exercise—For each fingerprint in the column (1–4), circle the matching fingerprint (A–D) in the corresponding row.

	A	B	C	D	E	F
1						
2						
3						
4						
5						
6						

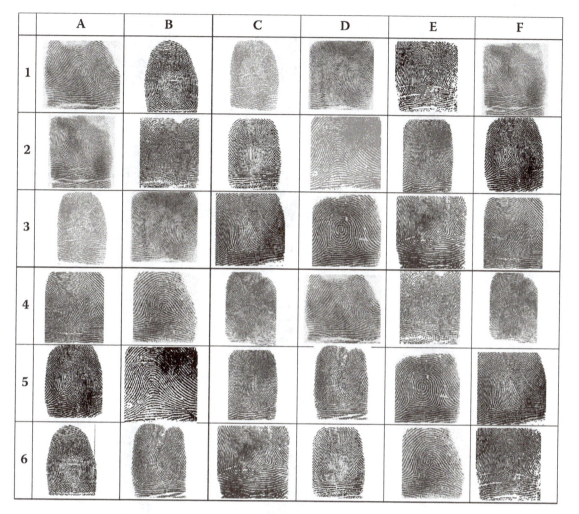

Figure 16.5
Part II: Fingerprint grid—Each fingerprint in the grid has one "matching" fingerprint. Indicate the grid location of the matching fingerprints.

- Figure 16.8
- Figure 16.9
- Figure 16.10
- Figure 16.11

Fingerprint loupe or magnifier (or scanner, computer, and image enhancement software)
    Fingerprint pointers (or scanner, computer, and image enhancement software)

16.3 Exercises

Part I: Fingerprint Matching Exercise

1. For each fingerprint in the column (1–4) of Figure 16.4, circle the matching fingerprint (A–D) in the corresponding row (Figure 16.4).

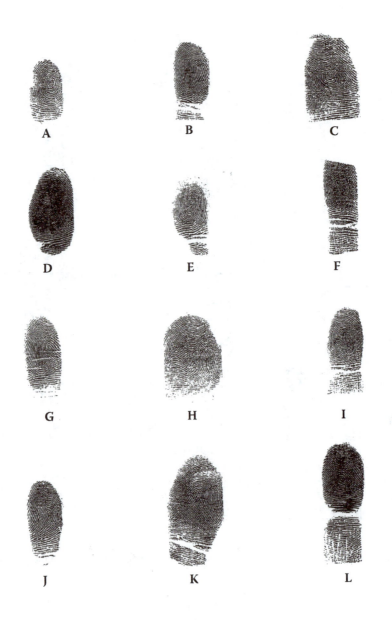

Figure 16.6
Part III: Fingerprint comparisons—Compare each of the fingerprints (A–L) with the known fingerprints in Figures 16.7–16.11.

Part II: Fingerprint Grid

1. Each fingerprint in the grid of Figure 16.5 has one matching fingerprint. Indicate the grid location of the matching fingerprints (Figure 16.5).

Part III: Fingerprint Comparisons

1. Compare each of the fingerprints (A–L) in Figure 16.6 with the known fingerprints in Figures 16.7–16.11 (exemplars 1–10) (Figures 16.6–16.11).

While the Miami Dade study found a 0% error rate when the verification phase of ACE-V was completed, all human endeavors have some probability of error. It would be more supportable to cite the error rate determined by the black box studies: 0.1%.[5] It is important to report the limitations of a scientific endeavor for the sake of honesty and transparency, as no science is infallible.

A statistical model is a quantitative calculation that can ensure accurate reporting and transparency of fingerprint identifications. Statistical models calculate the strength of an identification conclusion. For example, an "easy" latent print with 25 minutiae in common with an exemplar would have a higher quantitative value than a complex latent print with only eight minutiae in common with an exemplar print. There are currently no standardized, universally utilized statistical models for latent print comparisons. Several models have been proposed though multiple research projects are still exploring appropriate options. In the near future, statistical models will likely become a routine part of the fingerprint examination process.

In this laboratory exercise, minimum point standards, probabilities, and error rates will be explored.

17.2 Materials

- Pen
- Paper
- Figure 17.3
- Dice
- Figure 17.4
- Calculator

17.3 Exercises

Part I: Minimum Point Standards

1. Imagine you are a latent print examiner working for a forensics laboratory with a minimum point standard of six minutiae. In order to meet that minimum point standard for an identification, the latent print must have at least six minutiae in order to be deemed sufficient. Analyze each of the eight latent prints (A–H) pictured in Figure 17.3 and determine which latent prints meet your laboratory's minimum point standard.

2. Record the number of minutiae observed for each latent print, A–H.

3. Compare the number of minutiae you observed in each print with those of the entire group.

Part II: Exploring Probabilities—Rolling the Dice

1. Roll a pair of dice 100 times.

2. For each roll, indicate the sum on the dice with a tally mark in the appropriate row of Figure 17.4

3. Calculate the probability of rolling a seven by dividing the number of tally marks in the "7" row by 100. Convert the resulting decimal to a percentage.

4. How many combinations of di add up to a sum of seven? How many total combinations are possible? Divide the number of combinations that make seven by the total number of possible combinations. Convert the resulting decimal to a percentage. This is the true probability of rolling a seven. Is the percentage different from the results of rolling the dice 100 times?

Part III: Small-Scale Error Rate Study

1. Revisit the results from Chapter 16, Part III. Did you make any erroneous identifications? There were of a total of 11 possible identifications. In order to determine an error rate for the class, each individual should submit the total number of erroneous identifications and erroneous exclusions he or she made, anonymously.

2. When the total errors for the class have been counted, error rates can be determined. What are the error rates for the class? What is the erroneous identification error rate? What is the erroneous exclusion error rate?

17.4 Post-Lab Questions

1. In Part I, did everyone observe the same numbers of minutiae for each of the latent prints, A–H? What does this reveal about imposing a minimum point standard in professional case work?

2. What is the probability of rolling a "7" with a pair of dice? Did everyone calculate the same percentage? If not, calculate the error rate for the exercise. What percentage of individuals calculated a different percentage than the class consensus?

3. How was the erroneous identification error rate calculated in Part III? Is it higher or lower than the error rate reported from the large-scale fingerprint studies in the "Background" section above? Why?

4. Why is it important to report an error rate when testifying to a fingerprint identification in a court of law?

5. What is the benefit of determining the statistical strength of a fingerprint identification?

References

1. Daluz, H. 2018. *Fundamentals of Fingerprint Analysis,* Second Edition. Boca Raton, FL: CRC Press.
2. Polski, J. et al. 2011. The report of the international association for identification, standardization II committee. www.ncjrs.gov/pdffiles1/nij/grants/233980.pdf (accessed March 5, 2018).
3. Almog, J. and Springer, E. (Eds.). 1996. *Proceedings of the International Symposium on Fingerprint Detection and Identification*. June 26–30, 1995. Ne'urim, Israel: Israeli National Police.
4. Pacheco, et al. 2014. *Miami-Dade Research Study for the Reliability of the ACE-V Process: Accuracy & Precision in Latent Fingerprint Examinations*. Washington, DC: National Institute of Justice. www.ncjrs.gov/pdffiles1/nij/grants/248534.pdf. (Accessed October 22, 2017).
5. Ulery, B.T., Hicklin, R.A., Buscaglia, J., Roberts, M.A. (2011) Accuracy and reliability of forensic latent fingerprint decisions. *Proc. Natl. Acad. Sci. USA* 108(19): 7733–7738.

Chapter 18

Palm Print Comparisons

Objectives

- Understand the challenges inherent in latent palm print comparisons
- Recognize the common areas and features of the palm print
- Practice orienting and locating latent palm prints

18.1 Background

The purpose of comparing palm prints, as with fingerprints, is to determine whether an unknown print and a known print originate from the same source. ACE-V methodology is employed to analyze the level one, two, and three detail in latent palm prints. A latent palm print may be as small as a fingerprint or as large as the entire hand. The challenge when comparing latent palm prints is to determine their orientation and location within known palm prints. There are numerous patterns of ridge flow and creases within the palm. These common features are used to determine the location of interest and orientation of the latent though not every individual palm print will display every feature of ridge flow and creases shown in Figure 18.1.

There are three major creases that correspond to the flexing of the hand: the distal transverse crease (the top crease), the proximal transverse crease (the middle crease), and the radial longitudinal crease (the crease surrounding the base of the thumb). There are three major areas of the palm: the hypothenar (writer's palm), thenar (at the base of the thumb), and interdigital (below the fingers) areas (Figure 18.2). Each area of the palm comprises ridge flow that offers clues as to the position and orientation of a latent palm print.

The ridges of the hypothenar area are generally uniform and flow at a downward angle out the side of the palm. The hypothenar ridges funnel inward toward the center of the palm, while those toward the base of the palm flatten out like the base of a playground slide. A delta, known as the carpal delta, is present near the base of the palm. The carpal delta is an area where the ridge flow from the thenar meets the ridge flow from the hypothenar. The ridges in the thenar area at the base of the thumb flow in concentric half-moon curves that flow out of the base of the hand. As those concentric curves approach the base of the thumb, they flatten out and appear longer on top and shorter on the bottom.

The ridges of the interdigital area flow around four deltas—each associated with a finger. Below the index finger is an equilateral delta, each angle formed by the delta being approximately equal. Ridges from the equilateral delta flow at a downward angle between the distal transverse crease and the proximal transverse crease, through the funnel of the hypothenar and out the side of the hand. Ridge flow from the delta beneath the middle finger flows in a wave pattern along the top of the distal transverse crease and out the side of the hand. The deltas beneath the middle and ring fingers form acute angles pointing upward toward the fingers like martini glasses. The delta under the little finger forms an acute angle facing the center of the interdigital area, resembling a martini glass lying on its side. The ridge flow from these deltas often forms loop patterns.

The major and minor creases of the palm also offer orientation and location clues by their common paths and deviations. The distal transverse crease separates the interdigital from the hypothenar. It begins

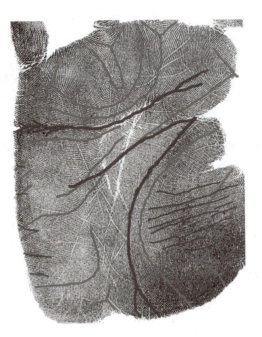

Figure 18.1
The common ridge flow and creases observed in palm prints are denoted.

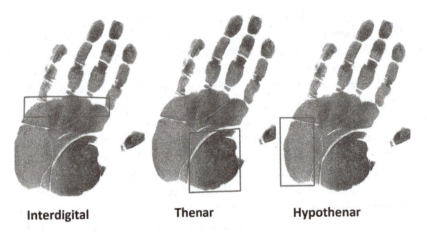

Interdigital   **Thenar**   **Hypothenar**

Figure 18.2
The three major anatomical areas of the palm: the interdigital area, the thenar area, and the hypothenar area (indicated with grey boxes).

at the edge of the palm where it displays a feathering pattern often called "crow's feet." It ends in the inter-digital area between the index and middle fingers, where it often forks, with one end of the crease ending at the equilateral delta below the index finger. The proximal transverse crease, located just below the distal transverse crease, begins between the thumb and index finger and ends in the funnel area of the hypothenar. Short, thin creases along the edge of the hypothenar cut across the flow of ridges.

The radial longitudinal crease begins between the thumb and index finger either below or adjoining the proximal transverse crease, encircles the thenar area, and ends at the base of the palm where it often branches along the thenar side of the carpal delta. The thenar may also have minor creases in a basket weave pattern across the surface, or horizontal, parallel creases. Edge creases in the thenar align with the ridge flow, rather than cut across the ridges as in the hypothenar. A feathered "starburst" pattern may also be visible between the thumb and index finger.

The second and third joints of the finger have many thin, vertical creases. The ridge flow of the middle and ring finger joints is generally horizontal and wavy. The ridge flow of the index and little finger joints slants downward, away from the middle and ring fingers.

In this laboratory exercise, the most common areas of ridge flow and major and minor creases of the palm will be observed. Latent palm prints will be oriented in the proper direction and their locations will be determined.

18.2 Materials

- Gloves
- Lab coat
- Safety glasses
- Pen
- Paper
- Fine-tipped dry erase marker
- Handiprint System® (8″ × 8″ white adhesive sheets with acetate covers)
- Black fingerprint powder
- Standard fingerprint brush
- Hand cleaner/wet wipes
- Figure 18.3
- Figure 18.4
- Plastic or glass plate (white or light in color)
- Black fingerprint power or magnetic black fingerprint powder
- Fingerprint brush or magnetic wand
- 4" fingerprint lift tape
- Large latent lift cards
- Fingerprint loupe and pointers (or a scanner, computer, and image enhancement software)

18.3 Exercises

Part I: Palm Print Creases and Ridge Flow

1. Record your lab partner's right and left palm prints with fingerprint powder using the Handiprint System (see Lab 5, Part II).

2. On the clear acetate cover of the right hand, trace the following creases and crease features using a fine-tipped dry erase marker. (Note that all features may not be present.)

   a. Distal transverse crease (forking and crow's feet)

   b. Proximal transverse crease

   c. Radial longitudinal crease (branching near the carpal delta)

   d. Edge creases in the thenar and hypothenar

   e. Basket weave or horizontal crease patterns in the thenar

   f. Starburst in the thenar

3. On the clear acetate cover of the left hand, trace the following features of the major areas of ridge flow in the palm using a fine-tipped dry erase marker. (Note that all features may not be present.)

    a. Interdigital area

        i. Deltas

        ii. Loops

        iii. Wave pattern above the distal transverse crease

        iv. Flow of ridges from the equilateral delta to the outer edge of the hand

    b. Hypothenar area

        i. Funnel area

        ii. Downward angle of ridges exiting the side of the hand

        iii. Carpal delta

    c. Thenar area

        i. Half-moon-shaped ridges exiting the base of the palm

        ii. Concentric curves approaching the thumb (flattened long ridges over short ridges)

Part II: Palm Print Location and Orientation

1. For each of the 12 latent palm prints in Figures 18.3 and 18.4, draw an arrow indicating the "up" direction.

2. Note the location of each latent palm print (the hypothenar, thenar, and/or interdigital areas).

3. Note the features present in each latent palm print, including the ridge flow and creases observed.

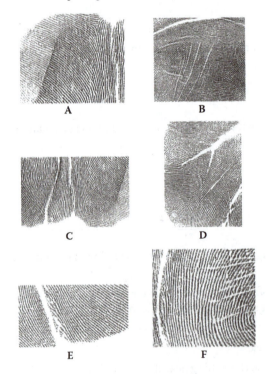

Figure 18.3

Part II: Palm print location and orientation—For each of the latent palm prints pictured (A–F), draw an arrow indicating the "up" direction; note the location of each latent palm print (the hypothenar, thenar, and/or interdigital areas); and note the features present in each latent palm print, including the ridge flow and creases observed (less complex).

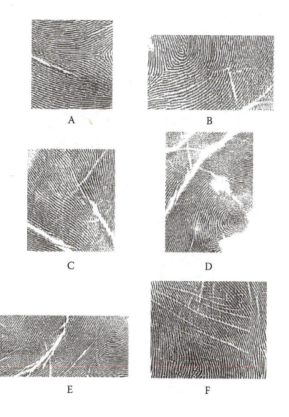

Figure 18.4

Part II: Palm print location and orientation—For each of the latent palm prints pictured (A–F), draw an arrow indicating the "up" direction; note the location of each latent palm print (the hypothenar, thenar, and/or interdigital areas); and note the features present in each latent palm print, including the ridge flow and creases observed (more complex).

Part III: Palm Print Comparisons

1. Use the wet wipes or a moistened towel to erase the dry erase marks from one of the palm print exemplars from Part I.

2. Have your partner touch a portion of his or her palm to the light-colored plate.

3. Process the plate with black fingerprint powder and lift the resulting latent print onto a latent lift card (see Chapter 10, Part I).

4. Label the resulting latent lift card with the mock case information provided.

5. Determine the proper location and orientation of the latent print.

6. Compare the latent palm print with the exemplar palm prints from Part I either manually (with a loop and pointers) or on a computer (with image enhancement software).

18.4 Post-Lab Questions

1. How are palm print comparisons similar to fingerprint comparisons?

2. What are the most challenging aspects of palm print comparisons as compared with fingerprint comparisons?

3. What are the names, locations, and features of the three major creases of the hand?

4. Which of the features of creases and ridge flow are visible in your palm prints from Part I? Which are not present?

5. What were some of the challenges with comparing the latent palm print to the exemplar palm print in Part III?

Chapter 19

Courtroom Testimony

Objectives

- Learn the role of the fingerprint examiner as an expert witness
- Understand how to be a successful expert witness
- Prepare a curriculum vitae (CV)
- Practice testifying as an expert witness in a mock court setting

19.1 Background

Forensic science is defined as any science applied to legal matters. Forensic scientists testify to their actions and conclusions in a court of law as expert witnesses. An expert witness is any individual who is more knowledgeable about a particular topic than the average person due to specialized education, training, and experience. Expert witnesses may testify to their opinions, while lay witnesses may only testify to what they observed or experienced.

Forensic experts must be able to explain their science and conclusions to a judge and jury in order to effectively communicate their opinions. Therefore, an expert witness is not only a scientist but also a teacher. Effective teachers are enthusiastic about the topic being presented. They present information in a methodical, systematic manner using plain language rather than excessive scientific jargon.

Visual aids, examples, and anecdotes are valuable teaching tools for fingerprint examiners. For example, simple line drawings of pattern types serve as an introduction to level one detail and the analysis phase of ACE-V. A line drawing of an ending ridge, short ridge, and bifurcation teaches the jury about unique characteristics within friction ridge impressions. Court charts such as Figure 19.1 are visual representations of fingerprint comparisons and assist the jury in learning the methods and processes by which a fingerprint examiner evaluates the minutiae to reach a conclusion. The use of anecdotes is another teaching tool that assists with jury education. For example, a latent print deposited on a substrate can be compared to a rubber stamp depositing an inked pattern on a surface.

The expert witness displays the qualities of an effective teacher as well as those of an effective public speaker. It is critical to make eye contact with members of the jury and speak with appropriate volume to be heard and understood throughout the courtroom. This ensures that the expert's enthusiasm and knowledge are communicated effectively. The successful expert witness is likable, acts naturally, and exudes confidence and competence. An expert's appearance and demeanor are also important. The expert must dress professionally in a conservative business suit and tie for men, pantsuit or knee-length skirted suit for women. Nothing should be worn or carried that may distract the jury: large jewelry, jangling coins or keys, heavy makeup, or bright colored clothing. Demeanor refers to the expert's behavior and manner. The successful expert witness exudes confidence and competence, regardless of nervousness or inexperience.

Another aspect to presenting oneself as a forensic professional is maintaining a professional curriculum vitae (CV). A CV is an extended resume: an autobiography of your professional life. It includes not only

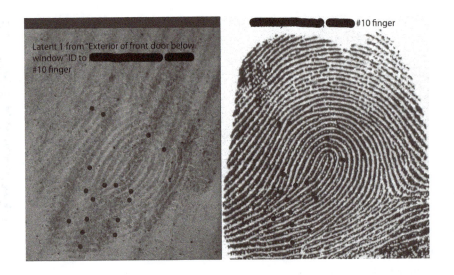

Figure 19.1
A court chart illustrates the comparison of a latent print (left) to a known print (right).

employment experience and education but also additional relevant scientific and technical experience. These additional sections may include the following:

- Employment/Experience (voluntary and paid)
- Professional development/Training (titles, dates, locations, trainers, and duration of each training)
- Presentations/Publications
- Association memberships/Affiliations
- Academic/Professional Distinctions/Recognition
- Equipment/Processes
- Court appearances
- Number of cases examined/Fingerprints compared (can be approximated)
- Specialized or proprietary software/Equipment/Processes utilized
- Other relevant categories: security clearances, languages, basic software proficiency

A CV is known as a living document, because it is constantly updated as new professional opportunities arise. Attorneys often utilize a forensic professional's CV when planning out their line of questioning during the *voir dire* of the expert witness. An opposing witness, hired by the defense attorney, may also use the examiner's CV to attempt to find weakness in their experience or training. It is therefore important to have a professional, up-to-date CV prepared prior to testifying in court.

Fingerprint analysts prepare for court by gathering and reviewing all case materials: photographs, case notes, laboratory worksheets, forms, and reports. Though most jurisdictions allow the expert to refresh his or her memory by consulting case materials on the witness stand, the expert should know the case well enough to refer to case materials only a few times, if at all. If the expert relies too heavily on the final report or case notes, it could appear that the expert is unprepared and erodes his or her credibility. If any errors are found during the case material review, those errors should be addressed and corrected immediately and submitted to your supervisor. A latent or tenprint comparison chart and other visual aids—such as a presentation with instructive slides for educating the jury—are also prepared prior to trial.

A pretrial conference is highly recommended. A pretrial conference is a meeting with the attorney prior to trial, the purpose of which is to educate the attorney about the analyses, results, your qualifications, and any weaknesses in the analysis. At a pretrial conference, the qualifying questions and the course of direct examination questions can be prepared. Any presentation or court chart prepared prior to testimony should be submitted to the attorney at this time, along with an updated CV.

On the day of court, the expert witness should leave enough time to park, go through security, find the appropriate courtroom, and check in with the attorney. When it is time to testify, the expert is called to the witness stand, takes an oath, then takes a seat, and organizes the case materials (Figure 19.2). The first phase of testimony is the voir dire of the witness, known as *qualifying questioning*. Fingerprint analysts answer qualifying questions in order to determine their competence as experts in their field. They are asked questions from the CV about employment, experience, education, training, knowledge of the history of the science and professional affiliations.

Direct examination is the second phase of expert testimony. During direct examination, the attorney who initially called the expert to testify questions the expert witness as to his or her actions, conclusions, and opinions. The expert recounts the evidence, analysis, results, and conclusions when prompted. Answers must be carefully considered and truthful. An expert who lies on the witness stand is guilty of perjury, which is a criminal offense.

Following direct examination, the opposing attorney has the opportunity to ask questions in a process known as *cross-examination*. The defense attorney asks questions in response to the direct examination to ensure the defendant receives a fair trial. The forensic expert must always remain unbiased. The defense attorney is awarded the same respect as the prosecutor. The role of a forensic scientist is only to interpret the science in a court of law not to have a stake in who "wins" or "loses." It is important to remember that cross-examination is not personal, and the expert should never get emotional, defensive, or angry on the witness stand. Doing so simply erodes the expert's credibility. The successful expert witness educates the jury; testifies to his or her actions, analyses, and opinions; and remains professional at all times.

In the following laboratory exercises, a CV will be created. Qualifying questions, direct examination questions, and cross-examination questions will be answered in a mock court setting. Figure 19.3 is a fictitious fingerprint analysis final report. You will answer questions as a fingerprint examiner for the Anywhere Police Department, where you have worked for one year. The use of anecdotes, narratives, and/or visual aids is encouraged.

Figure 19.2
Witness stand in a typical courtroom in the United States.

ANYWHERE POLICE DEPARTMENT
CRIME LABORATORY
LATENT PRINT SECTION
FINGERPRINT ANALYSIS REPORT

Latent Print Section	Case #2014-00214
1234 Somesuch St.	Agency: APD
Anywhere, VA 22000	Charge: Sexual Assault
(703) 555-1234 office	Investigator: (You)
(703) 555-1231 fax	Report Date: 02-19-2014

Items received:　　　#1 - beer can, 20 oz.
　　　　　　　　　　#2 – Pistol, 9mm, s/n ADP214
　　　　　　　　　　#4 – 8" strip of duct tape

Suspect: Morgan, John (dob 02-02-1994)
Victim: Doe, Jane (dob 06-11-1988)

The indicated items of evidence were received from the Anywhere Police Department Evidence Storage Section on June 10, 2014.

On June 10, 2014 items #1, 2 and 4 were processed for fingerprints using the cyanoacrylate fuming method followed by rhodamine 6G dye stain. One fingerprint (L01) was developed on Item #1. No fingerprints of value were found on item #2 or the non adhesive side of item #4. Item #4 was processed with black fingerprint powder suspension. Two fingerprints (L02, L03) were developed on the adhesive side of item #4.

The resulting latent fingerprints were compared to the above listed suspect and victim using ACE-V methodology on June 19, 2014. The results are as follows:

Item #	Latent Print	Identified to
1	L01	(v) Doe , #2 finger
4	L02	(s) Morgan, #1 finger
4	L03	no ID

The identifications were verified by H. Smith on June 19, 2014.

Figure 19.3
A fictitious fingerprint analysis final report to use in Part III and Part IV.

19.2　Materials

- Computer (or pen and paper)
- Figure19.3

19.3　Exercises

Part I: Writing a Curriculum Vitae

1. Create a CV using as many of the following categories as apply to you. Use examples from the Internet (or from *Fundamentals of Fingerprint Analysis, Second Edition*, Appendix D[1]) as a guideline to create the format of your choice.

   a. Name, current contact information

   b. Education (degrees earned, universities attended, locations of universities, dates of graduation)

c. Employment/experience (voluntary and paid)

d. Professional development/training (titles, dates, locations, trainers, and duration of each training)

e. Presentations/publications

f. Association memberships/affiliations

g. Academic/professional distinctions/recognition

h. Equipment/processes

i. Court appearances

j. Number of cases examined/fingerprints compared (can be approximated)

k. Specialized or proprietary software/equipment/processes utilized

l. Other relevant categories: security clearances, languages, and basic software proficiency

Part II: Pretrial Conference—Qualifying Questions

1. Conduct a "pretrial conference" with your laboratory partner, during which you discuss your qualifications as an expert witness. Answer the following questions, where applicable:

    a. What is your name?

    b. What is your occupation?

    c. Who is your employer?

    d. What is your job title?

    e. What is your current position at the Anywhere Police Department?

    f. What are your duties as a fingerprint examiner?

    g. What is your educational background?

    h. Do you belong to any professional organizations?

    i. Have you published any articles?

    j. Have you received any honors or awards?

    k. Have you been previously qualified as an expert in a court of law?

Part III: Direct Examination

1. Using the fictitious fingerprint analysis report (Figure 19.3), address the following direct examination questions with your laboratory partner taking turns to act as both attorney and expert witness:

    a. What are latent fingerprints?

    b. How are latent fingerprints made visible?

    c. What are known, or exemplar, fingerprints?

    d. How are unknown latent fingerprints compared with exemplar fingerprints?

    e. Is it possible for two people to have the same fingerprint?

    f. Why?

    g. For the case at hand, did you receive items of evidence to be examined for fingerprints?

    h. On what date did you receive this evidence?

    i. Where did you receive this evidence?

    j. How many items of evidence did you receive for this case?

    k. What were the item numbers for the items you received?

    l.   What is item #1?

   m.   What is item #2?

   n.   What is item #4?

   o.   Were you made aware of a suspect in this case?

   p.   What is the name of the suspect?

   q.   Did you receive exemplar fingerprints for the suspect?

   r.   Were you made aware of a victim in this case?

   s.   What is the name of the victim?

   t.   Did you receive exemplar fingerprints for the victim?

   u.   Did you process the items of evidence for fingerprints?

   v.   How did you process item #1?

   w.   Did your processing result in fingerprints on item #1?

   x.   How many fingerprints did you recover from item #1?

   y.   How did you label the fingerprints?

   z.   How did you process item #2?

  aa.   Did your processing result in fingerprints on item #2?

  bb.   How did you process item #4?

  cc.   Did your processing result in fingerprints on item #4?

  dd.   How many fingerprints did you recover from item #4?

  ee.   How did you label the fingerprints?

  ff.   Did you compare these latent fingerprints—L01, L02, and L03—to the victim and suspect exemplars?

  gg.   How did you compare the fingerprints with the victim and suspect?

  hh.   What were the results of your comparisons?

Part IV: Mock Testimony

1. In this exercise, you will testify as an expert witness in a mock trial. You will answer the qualifying questions and direct examination questions from Part II and Part III above, in addition to cross-examination questions posed by your instructor acting as a defense attorney.

19.4 Post-Lab Questions

1. What is the difference between a lay witness and an expert witness?

2. What are the qualities of a successful teacher and public speaker?

3. What are the three phases of expert witness testimony?

4. List and answer any other qualifying questions that may apply to your personal qualifications and experience other than those posed in Part II.

5. How can you improve your CV and/or develop your professional skills in order to become a more capable expert witness as your professional career develops?

Reference

1. Daluz, H. 2019. *Fundamentals of Fingerprint Analysis,* Second Edition. Boca Raton, FL: CRC Press.